Learning Support
a Guide *for* Mature Students

SAGE
Study Skills

Learning Support
a **Guide** *for* **Mature**
Students

Elizabeth Hoult

SAGE Publications
London • Thousand Oaks • New Delhi

© Elizabeth Hoult 2006

First published 2006

SAGE Publications Ltd
1 Oliver's Yard
55 City Road
London EC1Y 1SP

SAGE Publications Inc.
2455 Teller Road
Thousand Oaks, California 91320

SAGE Publications India Pvt Ltd
B-42, Panchsheel Enclave
Post Box 4109
New Delhi 110 017

British Library Cataloguing in Publication data

A catalogue record for this book is available
from the British Library

ISBN10 1 4129 0294 0   ISBN13 978 1 4129 0294 6
ISBN10 1 4129 0295 9 (pbk)   ISBN13 978 1 4129 0295 3 (pbk)

Library of Congress Control Number 2005930318

Typeset by C&M Digitals (P) Ltd., Chennai, India
Printed on paper from sustainable resources
Printed in Great Britain by The Cromwell Press Ltd, Trowbridge, Wiltshire

*This book is dedicated to my mum, from
whom I have learned the most*

Contents

Preface

This is a book about how adults learn and how we can use our abilities and experience to learn more effectively. It is written from a teacher's viewpoint and it is based on my experience of working with some startlingly successful adult students over the years. The inspiration for the book came from working with learners who stood out because of their remarkable ability to work on study programmes with great success despite everything that life threw at them – all manner of trials and tribulations beset their lives but they still managed to attend the college sessions, to complete the tasks at home and, ultimately, to succeed with flying colours. One such learner gave up her original career in her forties to re-train in a completely different arena. She described the process of learning as an adult as being akin to running up a downwards-travelling escalator. 'It takes a huge effort and it seems to go against all logic but it is hugely rewarding if you can do it successfully,' she told me. This made me question why it is that some people are able to do what seems so enormously difficult, and possibly illogical, and to succeed so spectacularly. What is it that these learners are able to do that others find so difficult and are we able to use their skills and insights to help all adult learners across the board? This book is an attempt to distil those strategies, skills and perceptions that lead to success and to make them available to the general adult learning population at all levels – for people taking evening classes at municipal adult education centres, returning to further education or embarking on higher education for the first time.

At the heart of the book are two assumptions. The first is that learning is a naturally occurring and wonderful thing that is central to what it means to be human. The second is that learning is both a cognitive and an emotional activity – the way that we feel is very much influenced by what we think and vice versa. I assume that you will have at least decided to think about embarking on a new course, if not started it already, if you are interested in this book. My aim is not to persuade you to start learning, rather to remind you why you have started and suggest ways to continue most effectively.

The models and concepts of learning in each chapter have been developed and adapted from a range of sources from the disciplines of education and psychology. Notes are provided at the end of each chapter on the inspirations for that chapter and these suggestions may be useful if you are interested in taking your understanding of the issues further. Although each chapter deals with a different aspect of learning and can be examined just from that perspective, the book has been written as a continual text and you will get the most out of it if you read it in a progressive way.

This book is written for adults who may be embarking on formal activities for the first time after a short or a long break. I say 'formal learning' activities because whether you realize it or not, you will have been engaged in learning activities throughout your daily life over the years. All of this is important and has a major impact on your learning and on the activities that are traditionally associated with study. You may be embarking on a foundation degree course or a professional qualification, in order to qualify as a learning support assistant, for example. If the latter is the case then you may find that your interest in the ideas covered in the book goes beyond improving your own capacity to learn and encompasses the body of knowledge that deals with learning and education as a discrete discipline. The suggestions for further reading at the end of each chapter have been included with you in mind and a full bibliography can be found at the end of the book. A number of psychological and educational models are covered within the text, ranging from personal construct psychology to behaviourism and motivational psychology. At times some of these theories are rather contradictory – a behaviourist approach to learning that suggests the incorporation of rewards into your study programme, it could be argued, is at odds with a constructivist view that suggests that you need to find ways of making the new knowledge mean something in your own context, for example. It is not my intention to suggest that you work exclusively within one theoretical field. As a teacher I find that picking from a repertoire of strategies is the most helpful way to enable learners to feel empowered by their learning and I have adopted this approach throughout the book. As you proceed through the text you will begin to get a feel for which ideas and strategies work best for you and you will be able to discard the others. The emphasis is on individualized learning so you can be the judge of what suits you and what does not.

This book is for you if you want to find out how to get the best out of studying, learn the secrets of successful learners and find out how to succeed. It will help you if you are already a confident learner and if you want to learn some practical ways of studying successfully. But it is also for you if you have lost your desire to study or if you feel that you never had one. Whenever we start a new project we experience a degree of anxiety. For some of us in certain situations, that anxiety is greater than others. The following chapters have been written to help you manage that anxiety and to put it to good use. Each chapter deals with a different aspect of learning, from how you use your mind most effectively to working with others in a way that best helps learning.

Included are individual self-assessment exercises. These will help you to gain a detailed understanding of your own particular strengths and weaknesses as well as your own motivation for starting and staying the course. These assessment exercises will help you to understand yourself better as a learner and as a person. By doing so you will be able to adapt material and activities to fit in with your own strengths and preferences and so make the most of the time available to you. They are not intended to be regarded as scientifically designed questionnaires that have been designed to give you an unrefuted, final analysis of yourself as a learner. Rather, they should be used as starting points for you to think about your strengths and weaknesses in the light of learning theory.

A note about the terms used. I alternate between the pronouns 'he' and 'she' throughout the book to demonstrate balance and I hope that I have avoided stereotypical portrayals of learners and teachers as a result. Three words – learning, course and study – appear repeatedly throughout the book. Learning is both a practical way of describing the activities that you are doing in order to study ('I am learning about Greek architecture', for example) as well as a much wider term used to encompass the process of change that comes about by anything that we do in order to add to or modify our current way of perceiving the world. Study is anything that leads to the furthering of this learning process – it can be literally 'studying' a text on your own in a room, or it could refer to the whole range of activities in which you take part, both those of your own choice and those set by your teachers. I mention the words 'course' and 'programme' fairly frequently as well. These words are used as shorthand to describe the formal, structured learning settings in which you are working – a degree programme, courses with other sorts of qualifications attached, courses with no qualifications attached that you have chosen to do for a definite, externally motivated reason, such as learning Spanish because you want to spend more time in vacations visiting countries like Spain and Mexico, or it may be that you are simply following your own 'course' of study in something that you are interested in for the pure enjoyment and satisfaction that it gives you – such as a particular period in art history or a type of English literature. Please remember that I use the words course and programme very widely in order to encompass all of these activities.

With this book supporting your learning you will have everything that you need to succeed. Let's get started.

Elizabeth Hoult

Acknowledgements

I am grateful to the following people who have helped me to develop this book: Simon, for his support and insight; Angela for her help with my understanding of the links between cognition, feelings and behaviour; Julie for broadening my appreciation of the mind and helping me to think about the teacher-student relationship in a more philosophical light; Christine for her comments on the draft; Patrick at Sage for his perceptive insights on work-in-progress; Hazel for helping me to develop my thinking about the links between personality type and reflective, independent learning; and Margaret for the tea, toast and desk in the final stages.

Most of all I would like to extend my thanks to the participants in the adult learners research project whose insights and observations about their own resilience as learners have considerably developed my own understanding of what it means to be a successful learner.

1 Why Are You Doing This?

This chapter will:

- Explain the benefits of learning
- Examine your own motivation for studying
- Look at the advantages of being an older – rather than a school-aged – learner

Learning is a good thing; its potential to improve a number of things in your life is enormous. Sometimes, though, it is difficult to remember what the benefits of learning are. At ten o' clock on a cold, wet January night when you are driving home after a boring class the benefits are not that obvious. Likewise, on all those sunny Saturdays when you would like to be at the beach with family and friends but instead have to spend the entire day under artificial strip lights in the library those benefits are not that obvious. Just because you have *chosen* to learn does not mean that you will always be keen to do so. The problem for many adult learners is the ever-present nature of the studying in their lives. 'Even when I take time off from swotting I am thinking about what I need to do next and worrying about the amount of work that I still need to get done,' as one put it. There is always the assignment that needs finishing, the wider reading for the project that needs to be done, or the connections that you need to make to your last piece of work, hanging over you like a rain cloud. It never ends. It might even be that you feel selfish in your decision to spend time studying, rather than time with others. To make matters worse, loved ones may even *tell* you that you are selfish – the last thing that you need to hear if you feel that you are already giving up so much in order to do it! So let's not underestimate the downsides of studying as an adult. It is challenging and the emotional, time and financial costs are significant. It is important to acknowledge this right from the beginning so that you do not feel like a failure when you experience periods of dejection and self blame.

Before we look at all the ways that you can improve your ability to learn and to complete tasks we will examine the phenomenal improvements that learning can bring to your life. Refer to this chapter when your morale takes a downturn. Research has shown that there are major benefits to the individual and to society in learning. Here are some of the most interesting ways that learning can enhance your life.

Benefits of learning

Research conducted by Hammond (2002) for the Centre for Research on the Wider Benefits of Learning has found positive correlations between learning, health and well-being. These include the following:

- Adoption of positive health behaviours, such as reducing smoking and drinking, increasing the amount of exercise taken and adopting a better diet

- Increases in occupational self-direction, self-esteem, self-fulfilment and financial security – all features of occupational success

- Development of autonomy, problem-solving skills, social competence and a sense of purpose and optimism for the future, which promote individual job fulfilment and good citizenship

- Promotion of social responsibility, social values and social skills, which facilitate social cohesion and positive involvement by individuals in the local community

The links between learning and life are complex and entangled but it is possible to assert that adult learning has a beneficial impact on our lives. In a separate article, Hammond, writing with her colleague Feinstein and Hammond (2004) argues that there might be six groups of reasons for these positive effects. These are:

- Changes due to the development of specific skills (such as IT)

- The effect of genuine cognitive development through specific learning

- Personal development through learning

- Peer group effects (just mixing with others regularly in a structured learning environment teachers us to be a better group member)

- Positional effects (mobility in terms of class and status)

- Economic effects (the old incentive of increased income)

They put the case for the link between adult learning and well-being powerfully (p. 217), 'Engaging in the common pursuit of learning under the direction of an experienced teacher, committed to developing co-operation and open discussion in a supportive environment appears to have all the ingredients for confidence building and raising social awareness'.

Learning can make you happier and healthier because by focusing on learning new skills and knowledge, you are able to think about your life in a fresh way and from a longer-term perspective and this encourages you to reassess other aspects of what you are doing. It could be argued that by imposing the structure on your life, learning shakes you out of old habits. Another school of thought is that the re-rejuvenating effect of learning means that by engaging in a cognitive activity (learning something new) you are literally creating new connections in the brain and that this makes the body behave in a way that it used to do when you were a younger person. Whatever the reason for it, the good news is that it happens.

Learning and self-esteem

As well as the physical health benefits, nothing else compares to learning as a way of improving self-esteem, and there is some evidence that, partly because of this, learning can have a preventative effect on depression. Ford (2005) explains how research into the effectiveness of an initiative that involved medical practitioners referring suitable patients for guidance and learning has shown positive benefits. The patients felt that learning made a difference to their lives, especially in terms of their mental health.

Mental health is closely linked to self-esteem. In order to understand what we mean by self-esteem it is helpful to think of ourselves as being influenced by two elements – the ideal self and the real self. The real self is our perception of where we are now – who we are and how we think that others see us. The ideal self is where we want to be or where we think that we ought to be – now and in the future. This will differ according to our own personal experiences and standards that we impose on ourselves and others. Low self-esteem occurs when there is too wide a gap between the two. Learning works in two ways to help us address this gap. First, it gives us the skills that literally allow us to get nearer to our ideal self. So, if having a degree is part of your picture of your ideal self then clearly by studying for one you will get closer to that view of yourself. Secondly, it helps us to challenge the assumptions that have helped us to create the ideal self in the first place. For example, I know very well that I do not look like a supermodel. I know that I never will look like a supermodel. Luckily for me I did not grow up in a family where physical perfection was regarded as the defining characteristic for excellence in women and girls. Other things were valued. Because of this there is not much space for physical perfection in my picture of my ideal self (although I wouldn't turn it down were it offered!). On the other hand, if I had grown up in a family where physical perfection for women and girls was not only revered but expected and if I then went to work in an industry – say fashion or pop music – that endorsed this view, then I might have a far tougher time in accepting that looking like a supermodel will never be part of my lifestyle! What learning does is that it offers us new perspectives on old assumptions and it offers us new dimensions to an ideal self. So if somebody else, who has grown up in a family where looks were valued above all else, takes up a course in combined sciences as an adult and finds out, much to her surprise, that she has something of a talent for physics, becoming an accomplished physicist is then incorporated into her view of her ideal self and suddenly not looking like a supermodel diminishes in importance.

Your ideal self

Learning adds new ways of looking at yourself to the ones that you have developed throughout your life. Look at the example below. It is from Helen – a student in her late thirties on an education part-time degree programme. She has made these lists in no particular order. Notice the way she has identified things that she is not particularly happy with in her life at the moment and articulated them in the first column. In the next column she has added the qualities that she would attribute to her ideal self – how she would like to be. Finally, in the third column Helen has added in the qualities and real skills that will be provided by her work for her degree – her learning self.

Case Study

Helen's real and ideal self

Real and perceived self	Ideal self	How can learning bridge the gap?
• Average achieving	• High achieving	• Knowledge that I can complete a course
• Career has stagnated	• New career direction	• Qualification
• Intimidated by clever people	• Confident in a variety of settings	• Meeting people through course
• Stuck in a rut	• Seeing things differently	• Education is a broadening experience

end of case study

Identifying for yourself, right from the beginning, what it is that you want to get from the learning experience will help you to think more broadly about what you are doing. People returning to education often answer quickly that their main motivation is a financial, career-based one – they want either to return to work or to change career direction. When questioned more closely, however, it becomes clear that they are also interested in the less obvious benefits to be found in learning. Ivan Lewis, a Parliamentary Under Secretary of State for Skills and Vocational Education in the UK Department of Education, talks about 'the dignity of self-improvement' (2005) in connection with adult learning, and this is of profound importance in the connection between self-esteem and learning. Another very powerful feature of learning is that it allows you to see beyond your own immediate perspective – it allows you to think more widely than just seeing things from your own small viewpoint and to develop an empathy with new ways of seeing the world. On a very practical level it provides you with a change of scene. It also imposes a structure on our lives in a new way that helps us to avoid the formless wallowing of depression.

Winning friends and influencing people

A commitment to education for its own sake is linked to a further commitment to make a contribution to society. A recent study of mature learners in London (Reay et al., 2002) concluded that mature learners value the fact that they are able to use their learning to make a difference to the lives of other people by drawing on their own, sometimes painful, life experiences and knowledge. The liberation and empowerment that comes from learning is very important to adult learners and for many this is linked to an altruistic desire to pass those things on to other people.

To put it bluntly, learning can make you a more open-hearted person. You may say that none of this really matters to you but it actually links to the earlier point about mental health. When we retreat into mental illness we tend to see the world as an increasingly scary, forbidding place. By taking up a learning activity and being informed by a community of learners we see more and more connections with our fellow learners and we are able to see more connections between ourselves and the outside world and to feel more hope than fear in our local (or national) context. By widening your perspectives and adding to your understanding of who you are and where you want to be, learning allows you to move beyond the confines of your own identity to a much wider understanding of the world at large. If you let it, the learning process can move you from an ego-bound (self-centred) position to one that is less separated from other people and more in tune with the exciting possibilities offered by the world.

Learning really is good for the mind and arguably it can act as a powerful antidote to mental weariness and illness. This is partly because it increases our ability to be in touch with our fellow humans and this is one of the most powerful determinants of well-being. Humans have evolved to operate in communities and, in general, isolated people are more likely to become depressed than those living and socializing with other people regularly. Learning helps to bring us into contact with new and interesting groups of people.

Learning and the workplace

Increased likelihood of advancement in the workplace or opportunities for a new job are often the reasons cited by adult learners for returning to study. West (1996) suggests that although mature learners say that these are their main reasons for returning to study, in fact their motivations are more complex and are actually linked to self-fulfilment and advancement in less obvious, personal ways than merely financial. There are certainly greater career development prospects associated with learning. Although in general this is most obviously true of learning that is associated with a particular job (such as management and accountancy courses) it is also true that people who are involved in ongoing learning activities that are recreational or purely academic are more likely to be financially secure than people who do not take part in such activities, but it is too simplistic to assume a causal link. In his account of a study of people aged over 45 who return to learning, Ford (2005) has shown that learning brings important benefits to people, including: the development of work skills to improve paid employability and equip them for volunteering and active citizenship; improvements in health and self-confidence; opportunities for social contacts; and strengthening of individual networks, including those that may lead to jobs.

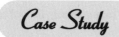

Case Study

Ian's story

Ian had been working in a fruit packing factory for six years. Although he enjoyed the companionship with his friends at work, the job itself bored him. As a reliable member of the team he had been promoted once to head of section, now the prospect of further promotion seemed to be the only way of his life advancing. Pondering the possibility of more responsibility but not relishing the idea of the rest of his life stretching before him in a job he did not like, Ian was in a dilemma. At about the same time that he was offered promotion, he enrolled in a night class in guitar playing. He had always enjoyed playing but had not played in a band since he was at school. He learned the various techniques of slide guitar and blues and set up a new band with other members of the course. Although he did not make much money from his music, his new found passion for it meant that he decided to accept the offered promotion because his hobby helped him to feel less frustrated at work.

end of case study

As you can see from Ian's story, the connection between earning and learning is often very indirect and unpredictable – Ian might have decided that the promotion seemed even less attractive as soon as he started to enjoy playing with the band and so he might have opted for a dip in salary in order to pursue becoming a professional musician. Indeed, you may decide not to pursue promotion or a career change at all but it might be something that you can think about when you need more motivation.

Learning and resilience

For all of us, the decision to take part in a new course of learning is enormously empowering. When we decide to do something and we stand by that decision then it has a great beneficial effect on our self-esteem. We can improve our self-esteem and understanding, independence, sense of purpose and hope, simply by taking part in a course that stretches us. And this is the main point: education can help us to solve problems and manage radical change, such as redundancy, divorce and bereavement, because it provides us with the skills we need to have in order to manage the situation as well as how to access help. One of the most enjoyable aspects of learning as adults is the new possibilities it opens up and the intellectual confidence and emotional maturity it brings.

So that is the good news. But if learning is so good for us, then why aren't we all doing it? The reasons are quite simple: it is hard work and it causes anxiety. This means that despite increases in uptake of adult education, you are still among the minority of the population by enrolling on a course – so you should feel proud of yourself for having the courage to do it. If a course does not challenge you then it is really not worth doing because learning is all about change, as we shall see as the book goes on. Learning is particularly challenging when you embark on it after a considerable gap in your life since you last put yourself in a formal learning situation. There is also a connection between the way you worked as a young person at school and the way that you learn as an adult. As such, your memories of school are both a rich resource and a limiting factor. Unlike when you were at school, there is now no rigid discipline structure in place to force you to study and the consequences of not working are only for you to consider. This has good and bad effects. On the one hand the learning can become a much more pleasurable experience, liberating you from punitive aspects of threats and detentions. On the other hand, it places enormous responsibility on your shoulders – ultimately, only you are responsible for your success or failure.

Case Study

Mary's story

Mary had been working for 15 years since leaving school with no qualifications. In that time she had been married, had two children and been divorced. She took a part-time job in her local primary school. She decided to enrol on a course for learning support assistants in schools following a suggestion by the head teacher that she should consider it. Nothing could prepare her for the prolonged period of anxiety that she would encounter from the moment she signed up until after she had passed the first year of her course. She lost sleep worrying about it and her health suffered. All the words of encouragement from friends and family did nothing to assuage her worries. At the back of her mind was the constant thought that she did not deserve to be there and that she was an impostor. This was her belief. It was only after Mary passed all her assessments in the first year of the course that she could relax enough to begin to allow herself to think otherwise. Reflecting on her feelings in her second and third years Mary began to appreciate the insights she had gained into the learning process and it has helped her enormously to empathize with the young learners that she is dealing with in the school.

end of case study

Mary's experiences will probably chime with you if you have re-embarked on learning after a gap. Her misgivings were psychological – it was her own sense of doubt that caused her anxiety. For many adults, though, there are real impediments to embarking on and continuing with learning. These are also real and tangible barriers that you may not have had to face as a child. Some of the most often quoted barriers to learning from non-adult learners are:

- **Feeling too old to learn**

- **Feeling nervous about going back into the classroom**

- **Concerned about not keeping up with the work and the group**

- **Feeling out of practice after such a long break**

- **Feeling like a fraud**

- **Feeling frightened of failure.**

All of these are very real reasons, but they are not insurmountable. We will deal with all of these perceived restrictions to learning throughout the book. There are also very real barriers to adults learning, such as:

- **Lack of childcare**

- **Nobody else to look after elderly relatives, disabled loved ones and pets etc. ...**

- **Poor public transport**

- **Lack of disabled access to the college/place of learning (including lack of support for visually or hearing impaired students)**

- **Lack of resources (to buy books or to gain access to computers, for example)**

- **Lack of funds to pay for tuition fees**

- **Intimidating recruitment procedures.**

Whilst not wanting to undermine the importance of these points, I will try to address ways of dealing with them throughout the book and I have included a list of contacts at the end of the chapter that might help with physical and practical impediments. The biggest single challenge that faces you as an adult learner is the sheer lack of time available. Another significant challenge is that you will need to re-learn some of the study skills that you may have lost over the years. We will deal with these issues as we progress through the book. Given the prevalence of these barriers it is vitally important that you feel secure in the learning situation. Educational achievement can enhance self-esteem which in turn motivates people to learn more. Self-esteem tends to be developed in contexts that are cooperative, challenging, inclusive and varied. In order to help develop resilience in learners, teachers need to give support and advice and to encourage participation and active learning. The safer you feel in your learning environment the more willing you will be to take intellectual risks and to enjoy learning for its own sake.

Motivation

Before you begin to think about strategies for success at your new learning activity, it is worth considering the ways in which you are motivated and what motivated you to start to study in the first place. Many things motivate us to embark on new enterprises. Some are external, such as the promise of more money, greater job security or promotion. Others are more particular to the individual, such as the pure enjoyment afforded by the activity itself and the satisfaction in doing it.

Motivation often starts with a need – a need for more money, more love, more security or more recognition, for example. Some of these needs are located at a very basic level and some at a much deeper level. However, the need often goes much more deeply than we think. We like to make meaning, and often the things that we are motivated to do and to learn come about because we have a very profound but basic human need to make sense of something that is chaotic, frightening or just confusing. It is a good idea to sort out for ourselves why it is that we do what we do in order to do it in the best way that we can. Complete the following self-assessment exercise and use your answers to determine what type of motivation applies to you and your reasons for undertaking your learning.

What is your motivation?

Answer A, B or C to each question

1   Which best describes your thoughts about the course?
A   It's a means to an end. I should get a new job out of the qualification that I will gain.
B   I really enjoy the sessions. I haven't thought about where the course will take me.
C   It's related to what I am doing at work, but that's not really my whole reason for doing it.

2   What do you most want to get out of doing the course?
A   A pay rise/new job.
B   New understanding of concepts and ideas.
C   New professional skills.

3   How do you see yourself at the end of the course?
A   In a better and more well-paid job.
B   Seeing things differently and understanding the world more clearly.
C   Doing the job that I am already doing more effectively.

4   When you hit a bad patch in your learning, do you?
A   Remind yourself of the career benefits.
B   Tell yourself that the difficulty is essential to the learning process and remind yourself of the good things about learning.
C   Understand that you will get over the difficulty and talk to other members of the group for help and support.

5   What do you most enjoy about the course?
A   Getting the good grades and passing each module.
B   The new understanding that I am gaining.
C   The satisfaction of learning something new and applying it to the workplace.

Count how many answers you have in As, Bs and Cs

(Continued)

(Continued)

Analysis of your Answers

Mostly As — extrinsic motivation

If you are extrinsically motivated it means that the rewards of learning, such as the pay increases and career prospects that will be associated with your learning, are what have attracted you to the course that you are working on/about to start. The motivation is variously described by psychologists as external to the person or external to the task. Your challenge is to be more flexible about the way that you see these rewards and not to disregard the accidental benefits of learning

Mostly Bs — intrinsic motivation

Lucky you! Some psychological theories of motivation suggest that this is the superior form of motivation because it comes from within and does not rely on shaky external factors for success. Intrinsic motivation is about finding strength within yourself and belief in yourself for what you are doing. You are less dependent on external rewards and are sustained by your own enjoyment and sense of fulfilment from the learning. Don't lose sight of other benefits to be had from learning and we will examine the ways that you can capitalize on these ideas in Chapter 9. Intrinsic motivation is used to describe the motivation for an activity that people engage in and derive satisfaction from the behaviour itself rather than the rewards that are linked to it.

Mostly Cs — intrinsic and extrinsic motivation

Most of us fall into this category a lot of the time and many motivational psychologists would say that both types of motivation interplay in our behaviour in reality, rather than strict divisions of either. Many adults who undertake learning activities tell a story about extrinsic motivation but in fact are much more intrinsically motivated than they realize. In fact, it doesn't really matter either way as long as you can compensate when your own motivation wanes.

It could be argued that an individual's belief in his or her own ability is a very good predictor of motivation. Therefore, in order to be motivated you need to develop your self-perceived strengths. Some people argue that the whole point of a compulsory (extrinsically motivated) education in the school-aged years is to prepare us as adults to embark on intrinsically motivated learning. Others argue that this is far too simplistic and that far from being rigidly divided into 'intrinsic' and 'extrinsic', both the type and degree of motivation vary at different points throughout our lives, as Becky's story illustrates.

Case Study

Becky's story

Like most of us, Becky has encountered both intrinsic and extrinsic motivation in various points in her life. At school she had an exceptional talent for art. This meant that she completed art homework for the pleasure of doing so and she was always involved and well behaved in art lessons because she was so absorbed with her work. In other words, she was intrinsically motivated to work in art. She went on to work in the marketing department of a chain of supermarkets. There she found many of the tasks that she was required to complete demanding and boring, by turns. She still worked hard, though, because her pay rise was contingent upon good performance and because she did not want her colleagues to regard her as lazy or not a team player. Becky started a course in lithography and commercial art in order to better her chances of promotion and to open up new career choices (extrinsic). There, she found herself enjoying it so much that her old, neglected love of art came to the fore again and she found a peace and satisfaction in working on her designs and mixing her colours that she had long forgotten. Her motivation, therefore, changed again from extrinsic to intrinsic motivation.

end of case study

Reflection and rest

As Becky's story shows us, the nature of learning and our reasons for learning tend to change considerably over time. The gaps in learning are not just intervals of time but also have their own important part to play in the overall learning process.

Contrary to what many of us were taught at school, some of the most useful learning insights happen when we are at rest and at play, rather than immersed in the task itself. In his important book *Wise Up*, Guy Claxton writes about the importance of 'soft thinking' 'One can learn to be more creative by cultivating states of mind that are relaxed and patient, yet quietly attentive and receptive to impressions, patterns and associations' (p. 154). Learning doesn't always happen in the immediate situation; usually it happens in the space and time after the class or course. This is why some of the best ideas occur to us after a class when we are in a supermarket or driving home. That's when we think, 'I wish I had said that in the class.' The point is though, that it was the discussion in the class and your conscious and unconscious reflection on what was said that led you to think that thought and have that insight. It is worth considering how you can integrate time and space for reflection into your life away from the formally taught parts of the course.

Age and experience

We live in a culture that celebrates youth to the extent that middle and older age groups often feel marginalized. Youth sells. Look at any typical slot of television advertising or at the way that blockbuster Hollywood and Bollywood films are cast and you could be forgiven for thinking that young people represent not only the majority of the population but also the only part of the population with money to spend. Of course this could not be further from the truth. The demographics in Western, capitalist countries typically mean that there are more and more older people with cash to spend – the direct opposite of the picture that we are presented with on our screens. Part of this myth of the power of youth is that only young people have the energy and mental agility to keep up with the rapidly changing world of information which we inhabit and that no other sort of knowledge counts any more. What rubbish! One's ability to understand a situation or a text, far from being diminished by age, is enhanced by it. All learning is based on experience and therefore the more experience we have the better equipped we are to deal with life and learning. This is the main benefit of being an older learner.

The main thing to remember is that the research shows that it is never too late to start to learn again. Lifelong learning offers opportunities for you, whatever your early experiences in the classroom were, and the good news is that you can develop new approaches to studying now that may not have been presented to you at earlier stages in your life.

Further Reading

- For more information about motivation you might look at Maslow's half-century-old but still relevant work on motivation as the pursuit of self-actualization (Maslow, A., *Motivation and Personality*, London: Harper and Row, 1954).

- There are plenty of sources of help available to you if practical impediments are preventing you from learning. If problems with childcare arrangements are preventing you from studying you might want to explore open, distance and flexible learning options. The advice that you will find at www.learndirect-advice.co.uk and the adult learning section of the government's main education site, www.dfes.gov.uk, should point you in the right directions.

- For students with special needs I strongly recommend that you visit the SKILL website at www.skill.org.uk. Skill is a national charity that promotes opportunities for young people and adults with any kind of disability in post-16 education and training across the UK. If you look at their website before you enrol on a course you can use their search engine to find your nearest college, check the level and quality of its disabled facilities and it will even give you the name of a disability advisor you can contact if any of your questions remain unanswered.

- You can read more about the wider benefits of learning research in the report by Hammond, C., *Learning to be Healthy* (London: Centre for Research on the Wider Benefits of Learning, Institute of Education, 2002). If you are particularly interested in the benefits of learning to the health and employment of people in middle age and older you should look at Geoff Ford's 2005 report *Am I Still Needed? Guidance and Learning for Older Adults* (Derby: Centre for Guidance Studies). This comprehensive report examines the policy situation surrounding adult learning and gives some good case study examples of places where learning opportunities work best.

- For more details about the Prescriptions for Learning initiative, in which patients were referred by medical practitioners for guidance and learning, look at Hughes, D., Bosley, S., Bowes, L. and Bysshe, S., *The Economic Benefits of Guidance* (Derby: Centre for Guidance Studies, 2002) and James, K., *Prescriptions for Learning: Evaluation Report* (Leicester: National Institute for Adult Continuing Education, 2001).

- If you are interested in reading more about motivation theory you will find the following collection of essays informative: Sansone, Carole and Harackiewicz, J.M. (eds), *Intrinsic and Extrinsic Motivation: The Search for Optimal Motivation and Performance* (San Diego, CA: Academic Press, 2000). In particular you may want to look at the chapter by R.M. Ryan and E.L. Deci entitled 'When Rewards Compete with Nature: The Undermining of Intrinsic Motivation and Self-Regulation'.

2 Intelligence and Ability

This chapter will:

- Provide a simple explanation of the learning process
- Introduce the idea that there are several ways of learning
- Explain why the popular view of intelligence is unhelpful
- Introduce the notion that we are able to think in different ways, according to the demands of a task

When most people think of learning they think of old style learning by rote – what used to be called 'learning off by heart'. This usually consisted of repeating something – a mathematical table or a few lines of poetry, for example – again and again until it stuck in one's brain. This is a skill that has diminished in importance, partly because fewer examination or curriculum documents call for it in the way that they used to and partly because advances in research into constructivist approaches to learning have meant that actually this form of learning is now regarded as somewhat superficial and inferior to deep-level learning that is characterized by a change in the learner's behaviour or understanding. That said, it is still a very important thing to be able to do in certain circumstances. Actors still need this ability to deliver lines on stage and any examination will call for a certain amount of rote learning even if this information needs to be applied to new contexts. The wider interpretation of learning is a more complex process that involves many more types of activities than the colloquial use of the word would suggest.

The learning process

Learning implies and involves change. Most typically, this will be a change in behaviour as a result of an experience – in formal settings this could be a study experience. This change could be a new-found skill or simply a new way of thinking about something. There are competing theories about how this happens. There are two ways of understanding the learning process. We can see it as the effects of external stimuli on the mind that produce particular results. The stimuli can either be positive (such as praise and rewards) or negative (such as deprivation or punishment). Alternatively, we could see learning as a process of gaining insights through socialization, the application of these ideas to 'real life' and the realignment of the original ideas accordingly. From your point of view it is not necessary to come down on the side of one theory or another, but you may want to bear both in mind when you construct learning activities for yourself and think about those that have been arranged for you. Two major changes have happened in the field of education in the past thirty years or so and both relate directly to you as an adult learner. First, there has been a significant reappraisal of what is regarded as intelligence. Secondly, it has become generally accepted that individuals are able to learn in rather different ways and that people may have strengths or weaknesses in particular areas.

We often, quite wrongly, reduce the learning process into two simple ideas – the subject matter or content of what is learned (the history of eighteenth century portraiture, for example) and the ways that we learn that subject – the processes that are often reductively known as 'study skills'. The latter description rather skims over what is a highly complex activity and it is worthwhile spending a little time really considering what it means to think about something and the different ways that we might think about a range of subjects. Learning happens when we bring experience and new information to bear on a situation or problem and apply the results in the future. Although this is a useful starting point it does not adequately describe all the unprompted thought processes that take up a lot of energy and which sometimes interfere with the problem-solving process and sometimes help enormously. Still, it can serve as a good working definition to use in this highly complex and difficult area.

How intelligent are you?

The answer to this question is two-fold: it is very difficult to reach a conclusive answer and it doesn't matter anyway. It used to be thought that we were all born with a fixed amount of intelligence or brain power and that amount was pretty much unalterable. This was known as our intelligence quotient (IQ). As Gardner explains (1999), the French psychologists Binet and Simon were approached by the French Ministry of Education in the early part of the twentieth century with the request that they should design a test that might help government officials to make statistical predictions about the levels of success or failure of the large numbers of children who were migrating with their parents to the French cities. The idea was exported to America, where instead of being restricted to an instrument used to measure patterns of success or failure it was quickly developed into a way of measuring individual strengths or weaknesses. As such the idea of the individualized intelligence quotient was born. This idea still holds a good deal of sway with some psychologists and educationalists and there are tests you can take in order to discover your own intelligence quotient. The average IQ score is said to be about 100. This notion of fixed intelligence lies behind the ethos of organizations such as MENSA as well as, indirectly, selective education systems such as grammar schools and the notion of 'elite' universities – the so called 'Russell group' universities in Britain and the Ivy League schools in the United States.

The idea is that our IQ is influenced by our genetic inheritance in the same way as hair colour and facial features are inherited from our parents. If one of our parents is talented then, it is argued, we are biologically pre-determined to inherit that intelligence, and the contrary if neither of our parents is academically talented.

Although this theory held a good deal of sway in the middle of the twentieth century and still has influence, there are major problems with it. First, the theory is not as 'scientifically neutral' as it pretends to be but is, in fact, culturally specific. The tests are dominantly based on mathematical and linguistic skills. These things can be taught and it is possible to increase somebody's IQ score with the right teaching, which causes big problems if we regard it as a true test of ability. Secondly, developments in child psychology have shown us that the influences of a child's brain are crucial in the first few weeks and years of life in determining how that brain develops. In other words, it is not the brain that we are born with that counts but how that brain develops in response to our experiences. All of this means that the notion of the IQ as something that is fixed and neutrally measurable is built on rather shaky foundations. The third problem with the notion of IQ is that it is very narrow in terms of what it actually measures. It measures an individual's ability to work with words, numbers and, to a certain extent, spatial concepts, but it ignores all the other types of intelligence that are required to, say, create a beautiful picture or to win a gymnastics competition and this leads me to the next point – the existence of multiple intelligences. The possession of a high IQ score does not in any way guarantee one's ability to think independently or with integrity or to be flexible or appreciate beauty – it simply records one's ability to score well in an IQ test. Tony Buzan (1974) tells us to regard IQ tests as 'games or "markers" of a current stage of mental development in a few specified areas'. In other words, they have their uses but should not be regarded as the ultimate indicators of our intellectual worth.

Different kinds of intelligence

Among others, Gardner (1999), the eminent cognitive psychologist, has argued that far from there being just one intelligence, there are perhaps as many as nine types. These include: linguistic; mathematical; spatial; naturalistic (which enables human beings to recognize, categorize and draw on features of the environment); interpersonal (the ability to relate to and empathize with each other); intrapersonal (the ability to recognize and name our emotions and to 'manage' our feelings); musical; and bodily-kinaesthetic. Another possible type of intelligence is loosely known as existential intelligence – this is a concern with the bigger questions about life – and the linked concept of moral intelligence – a contentious concept because we have no fixed definition of what morals are. As an older learner you clearly have access to many more experiences that allow you to develop the emotional dimensions of intelligence – interpersonal, intrapersonal, existential and moral intelligences. This makes the work of Gardner helpful and potentially liberating for adult learners and, for all of the criticisms of his detractors, it is a useful starting point for discussions about how to get the most out of learning situations. He has developed a battery of tests that can help you to understand where your strengths lie. He also argues that not only does it benefit the learner to understand what strengths she has but also that as a society, and especially the educational establishment, we need to reappraise our understanding and categorization of intelligence to incorporate a much wider view. As with all the different categorization methods for learning styles and intelligences, it is very important to remember that they are not genetic blueprints and that they represent indications rather than prophecies for behaviour in any given learning situation.

Different ways of learning

Along with the work in the late twentieth century that went into creating a new understanding of intelligence there has also been a good deal of development in the understanding of the process of learning. Not only do we all have intelligences in differing degrees but they have a big impact on how we learn and we all learn differently.

Linked to the theory that there are multiple intelligences is the idea that we all learn according to our own particular strengths and weaknesses. That is to say, that there are particular differences in the configurations of our minds which mean that we process information differently and that there are ways of working that we prefer over others. There is much debate about whether these differences are innate (we are born with them) or if they are a product of conditioning (we acquire them through experience), but the argument goes that we are all subject to these individual differences and therefore it is beneficial to all of us to understand what our personal learning style preference is and to organize our work accordingly. In the end, it does not really matter what we think about where these preferences 'sit' or about whether or not they are 'real'. The concept is only useful in so far as it makes the learning process more accessible for us, all other discussion of their existence is purely academic. If you take a skill such as learning how to drive a car you can see that an over-reliance on the preferred learning styles and multiple intelligences theories would be of limited value in the long run for the learner driver. Imagine a learner who has discovered that her dominant strengths are linguistic and interpersonal and therefore she aims to adapt all information to herself in this way. As such she might read a book about learning to drive a car and develop effective relationships with other car drivers and her driving instructor. All of this is of limited use to her until she is able to actually get into the car and drive it. So her other sources of information are fine as peripheral, supplementary skills but until she actually has the opportunity to get behind the wheel of the car, they will remain redundant.

Theories of learning style preference

The first notable thing about learning style theories is how many of them there are, and it is worth saying at this point that there are many competing ideas about the value and validity of each theory and that none is the 'right' one. The aim for all learners, whatever their style, is to build up a wider repertoire of learning styles so that they can become effective learners. Effective learners generally are able to learn from mistakes and to stick with a study programme even in the most trying circumstances. Here are some of the characteristics displayed by effective learners:

- **Able to try out different types of academic tasks**

- **See themselves as the main agent in the learning process**

- **Demonstrate understanding of the prior context and are able to apply that understanding to present learning**

- **Understand that learning involves anxiety and are not daunted by that anxiety but instead use it to enhance the learning**

- **Able to focus on a long-term goal and to incorporate the challenge of the new learning situation into the understanding of the bigger picture**

- **Able to select the specific strategies from a repertoire of methods and techniques**

- **Able to draw on their personal and life experiences to reflect on academic problems and develop independent and self-confident approaches to new situations and subject matter**

- **Resilient and reflective.**

So, these eight points describe what you are aiming for – it is up to you how you go about achieving it. Multiple intelligences and preferred learning styles theories are not ends in themselves – simply routes towards becoming an effective learner.

All of this means that before we go any further you might find it useful to try to gain a good understanding of your particular learning style in order to see how you can use it to your best advantage in your learning. To return to our learner driver, once she has created the opportunity for herself to learn how to drive, she can then employ what she knows about her strengths and weaknesses to break down information given aurally into small chunks and to spend some time working out what the diagrams and pictorial representations in the driver's handbook mean so that she can transcribe them into verbal information. She will only learn effectively, though, if she can apply this new information to old knowledge and to make sense of her current context.

Working with your mind

The brain is an incredible piece of equipment – so powerful that even with all the scientific advances of the twentieth and twenty-first centuries, there is still much more that we do not know about the brain than what we do know. Given its awesome power and complexity, it is curious that we do not spend any time at all in learning how to use it and work with it. Instead we see ourselves as slaves to our brains, subject to each uncontrolled thought that it throws up and victims to the way it runs wild. In Chapter 1 I explained that not all learning is formal learning and if you pause for a minute to consider all the things that you have learned informally you will be staggered by your brain's capacity to learn. Think about phobias or other irrational anxiety conditions, for example. No explicit teaching has gone into somebody's fear of trains, for example. It probably may have only taken one episode or a single bad experience and even that may have been a vicarious one – hearing a story of how dangerous trains can be from a parent in a sufficiently colourful way would be enough to trigger an extreme response in a vulnerable person and for the phobic person to develop their fear. This shows you how rapidly the brain can process information when it has to and how fearsomely it holds onto that information once it is there. The learned behaviour, if unchecked, can go on to have a profound effect on the way that the person defines himself, thinks and, ultimately, lives his life. Clearly, the development of an irrational fear of trains is not helpful for the commuter and so the challenge is how to turn this tremendous capacity for learning into a helpful experience. There is a very good case to be made for learning to manage our minds and not be managed by them. Try to see your thoughts as products of your mind rather than *being* your mind. You will find some practical ideas which are designed to help you to gain this distance in Chapters 4 and 5.

There is a very close relationship between personal, professional and academic development. Learning is never just about gaining new knowledge: it involves becoming something new. You are never just the passive recipient of transmitted knowledge because as a learner you are also a human being who changes as a result of what you know. This means that a mechanistic concentration on study skills that assumes that we can simply apply ready-made tools to any situation will always be limited by its assumption that we are all the same. Instead, we need to take a step further back and consider the ways in which we access and process knowledge in the first place.

How do you prefer to take in information?

The following self-assessment exercise is designed to help you understand how you learn best as an adult. It has been adapted from the work on visual, auditory and kinaesthetic ways of learning put forward by Rose (1985) and Dunn and Dunn (1978) among others as well as being influenced by Gardner's afforementioned work on multiple intelligences. Complete the exercise and then look at the answers, which will give you a basic understanding of how you prefer to take in information. We will use the diagnosis as a starting point for finding out how you see learning in general and are able to get the best out of all learning situations.

How Do You Prefer to Learn?

Answer A, B, C or D to each question

1   You know that you will be making a journey to a wedding in a place that you have never been before. It is important to you to be on time so you need to get directions before you go. How would you prefer the directions to be presented to you?

A   In the form of a conventional map – perhaps with the route highlighted in coloured pens.

B   In clearly written bullet points with no map accompanying the directions (for example, 'At the end of the road turn left where you will see a sign pointing to the church … etc.')

C   By listening to well-spoken instructions from somebody you trust that you are able to memorize – a real luxury would be to have the instructions on tape or spoken from a computerised GPS system in the car.

D   You would never rely on luck for such an important event. You would have made a special effort to do a practice run first – you have to know how the journey feels – remembering each twist and turn – before you can commit it to memory.

2   You are meeting a delegation of guests to your town from a foreign country. They speak a language that you have never learned before but you want at least to show them that you want to learn more about their culture and you ask them to teach you a couple of common courtesies in their language. How do you learn the words most easily?

A   By seeing a picture of what the word is describing at the same time as it is spoken – for example a picture of shaking hands when the word for 'hello' is uttered.

(Continued)

(Continued)

B By seeing the word itself written down in the foreign language – with the translation in your own language directly beneath – when the word is spoken.

C You pick it up quite easily just by listening to how it is spoken and repeating it.

D You are helped enormously by doing the accompanying action – for example shaking hands as you say the word for 'hello' and nodding your head slightly when you say the word for 'thank you'.

3 You need to go shopping but you have come to the shops without the list that you made the previous evening so you have to remember everything that you need. How do you do this?

A By picturing each of your partially empty cupboards at home and buying what is needed to fill the spaces.

B By picturing the list itself – or as much as you can remember of it.

C By saying a couple of the items that you can remember aloud – it jogs the memory for the rest.

D By thinking about the week ahead and how you will need to buy things to satisfy your hunger etc. and sort out the stain on the carpet – you imagine yourself kneeling down to work on the stain and feeling hungry after doing the late shift on Tuesday evening, for example, and buy your purchases accordingly.

4 How would you best like to learn about a historical event?

A By visiting a photographic or art exhibition about it.

B By reading a well written article about it.

C By listening to an inspiring lecturer (on the radio or real life) discuss the events.

D By visiting an historical place associated with the event (such as a battleship or a stately home) and getting a feel for the place and the events that happened there – smelling and imagining what it must have felt like to be there at the time.

5 You are planning to go on holiday or to visit a new area for the first time. You are interested in getting a feel for the place before you go. How would you choose to do this?

A By studying maps and pictures of the area.

B By reading guide books and articles about the area.

C By listening to the music of the area and talking to people who know about it.

D By getting a feel for the culture – perhaps by sampling the sorts of foods that might be available out there.

(Continued)

(Continued)

6   You have set yourself the challenge of learning how to cook quite a complex meal. How would you prefer to do it?

A   To have a picture of the finished article with staged instructions with diagrams to take you through the process.

B   Through a traditional recipe book.

C   By listening to instructions – on the radio or from another person.

D   After reading some initial instructions using your own common sense to estimate the quantities and relying on tasting the meal at every stage to guide you through the process.

7   You have plans to re-decorate your living room in a new colour scheme. How would you go about the process?

A   You love this sort of activity – you will have a good look at source books for ideas and match the colours to give the right appearance and then throw yourself into the process.

B   The whole process bores you. You like looking at magazine articles about styles and colour schemes but when it comes to doing the job you do your utmost to find somebody else to do it!

C   Your taste is quite conservative but you find the process very restful – you like nothing more than a couple of days with the radio on as you do the painting.

D   You are fine as long as you understand what the room is used for and have a feel for what it is going to be like. You may not be the world's most creative interior decorator but you have a very steady hand and you enjoy the physical process of painting.

Count how many answers you have in As, Bs, Cs and Ds

Analysis of Your Answers

Mostly As

This preference is for taking in information **pictorially**. If this is your style then you probably work very well with images – maps pose no problems for you and you enjoy looking at photographs and diagrams in order to make sense of a subject. This is a great advantage for you if you are studying subjects that rely on a high concentration on visual information. When you are studying for subjects without this amount of visual stimulation you might consider finding ways of integrating it.

(Continued)

(Continued)

For example, you might want to draw images of ideas that you want to incorporate into an essay, before using them to construct a plan that might be arranged in different coloured sections to show your thought progressions. It might also be worth your while to find accompanying visual images to help you to process and remember new chunks of information. If you are learning about an abstract concept – such as romanticism in literature and poetry – it will be of enormous help to you to know how the movement manifested itself in painting and by looking at works by Turner you will get a better understanding of the concepts described. The knowledge that you deal with visual images particularly well may also persuade you to incorporate visual presentation of complex information in your own work – try using graphs and diagrams to illustrate your ideas as well as written text, for example. Mind mapping (see the suggestion in the further reading section at the end of this chapter) may be particularly useful for you.

Mostly Bs

This preference is for taking in information **textually** – through the written word. This is good news if you are working on a course that involves a good deal of reading and writing. You will thrive on textual work and you may feel that you need to annotate books – or underline key points. You will probably have the feeling that you don't really get to know about a subject until you have written about it. You may find working with maps and graphs quite difficult, by contrast, and you may feel completely lost when you have to take in information purely aurally, without any written prompts. You may have had the experience when working with a second or third language that you need a word repeated several times before you can fully take it in and repeat it. When dealing with a written version of another language you may feel much happier, though. You may want to consider incorporating written work and reading texts into other types of work. Creating your own study diary – to run in parallel alongside the rest of your assignments – may be of great help when you are in study situations that provide scant opportunities for working with the written word. You can also capitalize on your ability to interpret texts by reading supporting materials for any abstract subject. So if you are working on geographical phenomena such as river erosion, for example, and having to deal with a lot of graphical representations (diagrams, cross-sections of river channels and photographs as well as statistical graphs representing erosion rates), then support your understanding of the concept by reading around it – in textual explanations of the phenomenon. Also, you might want to 'pin down' your knowledge as it progresses by 'translating' the visual images into your own words and attaching a statement to each of the images.

(Continued)

(Continued)

Mostly Cs

This is a way of working that prefers to process and remember information in **audio** forms – in other words, learning by hearing and talking. You have probably already noticed that you are able to 'pick up' points very quickly in lectures. You are also quick off the mark with your responses to what is said to you in conversation. You can recognize tunes and people's voices rapidly and you may find that you are able to understand foreign languages quite quickly – more quickly than other people if you are all in a new country together. The downside of this way of learning is that you may find staring at stationary, silent images – such as pictures and texts – rather boring and difficult. This is a nuisance if your chosen path of study involves a lot of reading and examination of figures and diagrams. There are many ways that you can capitalize on your strengths. Try to use your own voice to help you to commit ideas and facts to memory – invest in an mp3 player or a tape recorder so that you can record yourself reading from notes or a text and then play it back to yourself like a lecture. You may also find that you are able to make good use of a dictaphone. This useful piece of equipment will enable you to make an audio collage of your early ideas about an assignment – simply speak all your ideas into the dictaphone as they occur to you. Then, as you play it back, try to order them using images or text. So if you have been asked to write an assignment about religious festivals use the dictaphone to record all of your immediate and deeper thoughts about the topic. Don't rush this – the longer that you spend on it the better it will be. Do not try to censor your ideas at this stage – you can do that later. The point of the exercise is word association so the more links that you can make in your imagination the better. Now you can either play it back or make a plan on a piece of paper or your computer – as described above – or you can listen to it again – just jotting down the most important ideas. Using this *aide-mémoire* you go back to the dictaphone to structure these ideas into a more detailed plan. There is some evidence that the use of music can be beneficial for certain kinds of intellectual endeavour. To this end you might want to experiment with using background music (but not a radio station that has a lot of talking as part of its output because this will distract you) to help you to work when reading and writing.

Mostly Ds

This learning style is what we shall call the **action-orientated** preference. It means that your mind–body connection is particularly close and that physical experiences help you to learn. You learn best by feeling what it is like to smell, taste and move in the ways that the subject matter dictates. You probably have very good hand to

(Continued)

(Continued)

eye co-ordination and you are able to remember dance moves reasonably easily. The downside is that you may feel bored and restless when working on more stationary pursuits such as reading and writing and listening to lectures. There are ways that you can use this preference to enhance your learning of even the most bookish of subjects. The main thing is to incorporate movement of some kind (real or imaginary) into your thinking about a topic. So if you are working on writing a response to the poetry of Shakespeare you might walk up and down in the rhythm of the lines of text. The field trip was made for learners like you – try to build in opportunities for yourself to go to places (museums, foreign countries, geological formations, etc.) to actually experience what the knowledge means in situ. If you are writing a discursive essay about a contentious issue – such as the use of fossil fuels – you might want to write your thoughts down on separate cards, rather than one piece of paper. Then, as you develop your ideas about the reasons for and against increase in the use of fossil fuels you can literally move the cards around to demonstrate the opposing points of view. You may feel deprived if you simply restrict your learning to the times when you are sitting on your own in silence at your desk. So try to incorporate your learning into your daily activities – particularly walking.

Using your learning style preference

The categories above should give you some idea of where your strengths lie. If you read through all of the descriptions you may also have some inklings of where your weaknesses might be. There are two ways of using the information.

1   **You can do your best to adapt as many learning situations as possible to ones that incorporate your learning style. So, for example, you find ways of replacing text with pictures and diagrams if you are a pictorial learner.**

2   **Alternatively you use the understanding of where your strengths and weaknesses lie to manage your time more effectively. It will be impossible to expect all the information that you need to be presented in your own preferred way. But when you are faced with a situation where you need to work in the opposite way that you would choose to do (say you are a text-based learner who needs to learn in an action-orientated way, in the process of learning to drive, for example) you can use the knowledge of your preference to allow yourself more time and to be**

kinder to yourself when you find those activities more difficult. Go through the test again and this time indicate the worst way of working for you in each category – this will give you your opposite type and an indication of the situations that you will find the most challenging. In some ways this information is the most valuable.

It is important to remember in any discussions about learning style preferences that they are just a construct – a way of seeing and categorizing the world that makes it understandable to ourselves. They are not 'real' in the sense that we have a gene that makes us, say, a text-based learner and nothing else. Rather it indicates the way that our mind has developed over a number of years and it describes the way that we prefer to work – given a number of options. It does not mean that we cannot work in any of the other ways and indeed it is useful for us to continue to develop these other skills all the time – but it does mean that we probably find the other ways of working quite hard. So this is information that you can use to enhance your studying – it can allow you to make the most efficient use of time and to work in the most productive way.

Study plans for the learning style preference

Preference A: the pictorial learner

Do:

- **Try to find ways of representing information given to you in other forms as pictures, diagrams and graphs**

- **Try to find existing representations of knowledge in these forms**

- **Use mind maps and coloured spidergrams to revise and plan for assignments**

- **Make use of educational films and programmes to enhance your knowledge.**

Don't:

- **Involve yourself in prolonged work with pure text and no images**

- **Rely on radio or audio tapes as the main form of learning**

- **Beat yourself up when you become bored or tired when no visual images are to hand.**

Preference B: the textual learner

Do:

- Make as much use of the library as possible

- Opt for essays and dissertation writing – it is your strength

- Use a learning journal or study diary – even if the tutors have not asked you to do so – it will help you to document your learning.

Don't:

- Rely entirely on visual information

- Listen to a lecture without making notes – even if you never go back to the notes you at least have made new connections by writing the words down

- Do anything without incorporating some text – even with a purely physical task try to make some notes about it.

Preference C: the audio learner

Do:

- Use tapes and dictaphones to help you to remember knowledge

- Explore the use of classical music to work with

- Make as much use as possible of conversations with other learners.

Don't:

- Chain yourself to the desk and sit in silence while you study

- Miss opportunities to give yourself aural cues to jog your memory.

Preference D: the action-orientated learner

Do:

- Use movement and dance to help you to remember things

- Get up and move around every so often as you are learning

- Try to visit real sites of knowledge in order to add depth to your learning.

Don't:

- **Get into too many situations where you are working exclusively with text on your own**

- **Get into too many situations where you have to sit still and listen to somebody speaking in an unsupported way. Build breaks in for your self (even by walking in and out of the room between lectures) to help with this.**

Further Reading

- If you are interested in the notion of multiple intelligences and would like to read more about it, Howard Gardner's work is certainly a good place to start because it is written for a wide audience. His self-assessment inventories are fun to do and can provide you with a sharper understanding of your own strengths and weaknesses than the outline given here. His 1993 version of the theory can be found in his book *Frames of Mind: The Theory of Multiple Intelligences* (London: Fontana Press). You might also be interested in the work of Tony Buzan about mind-mapping if you find that visual representation of ideas works for you. His book *Use your Head* (London: BBC Books, 1974) is worth a look. Buzan is credited with inventing mind mapping, including methods for rapid and effective note taking, thinking and cramming for exams.

- If you are interested in pursuing the idea of learning styles you could look at a range of texts, including Honey, P. and Mumford, A. *The Learning Styles Helper's Guide* (Maidenhead: Peter Honey Publications, 2000) and David A. Kolb's work *Experiential Learning: Experience as the Source of Learning and Development* (Upper Saddle River, NJ: Prentice Hall, 1984). The latter argues that the four main ways of learning are concrete experience, reflective observation, abstract conceptualization and active experimentation.

- John Dewey's arguments about learning as a natural activity for human beings have had a good deal of impact on adult education ideas. His important work *Experience and Education* (New York: Collier Books, 1963; originally published in 1938) is a good read. He argues that effective learning connects experience with the subject being learned and that for the adult educator, helping adult learners to recognize the strength of their own previous experiences is quintessential to their progression.

- There are many theoretical approaches to learning but a good, short paper that provides a thoughtful and accessible conceptual overview is Watkins, C., Carnell, E., Lodge, C. and Whalley, C., 1996 *Effective Learning* in the National School Improvement Network's 'Reasearch Matters' series of pamphlets (London: Institute of Education, Summer, 2002). The authors demonstrate that learning is an active process in which learners link new experience to existing meaning and may accommodate and assimilate new ideas as they do so. In the learning process past, present and future are connected, although this connection may not be simplistic or linear – people continue to unlearn and re-learn as they go along. They also stress that the intended future use of the learning is essential to the success of what is currently being learned.

- The work on visual, auditory and kinaesthetic approaches in this chapter is a highly simplified adaptation of the work of Dunn, K. and Dunn, R., *Teaching Students through Their Individual Learning Styles* (Englewood Cliffs, NJ: Prentice Hall, 1978). Their Learning Styles Questionnaire is comprised of 104 questions about a range of environmental, emotional and physical factors, of which visual, auditory and kinaesthetic are just one element.

3 How Do You Learn Most Effectively?

This chapter will:

- Consolidate the ideas from Chapter 2 and help you to apply them to your own learning
- Give you an indication of your own preferred ways of working and the wealth of knowledge that you already have at your disposal
- Help you to use your understanding of your own preferred ways of working to construct a study plan

Personal learning

As we saw in Chapter 2, there has been a great deal of interest in the past few years about the idea that we all learn in different ways, with advocates of this view arguing that we all have particular configurations in the ways that we think (that may be innate or they may be the result of particular conditioning experiences) and that these mean that our brain is 'mapped' in a way that predisposes us to particular ways of learning and dealing with information. Adversaries of the view argue that this is merely a construct – a theory – that has been imposed on the highly complex business of learning by academics who have little evidence for the phenomenon other than that they think it happens. It is of little importance for adult learners whether this is 'true' in the scientific sense or if it really is just a theory. The point is that it can be enormously helpful when we are learning because it provides us with a way into a challenging process and it helps us to identify and play on our strengths. So we will use the basic idea that there are different ways of accessing and processing information and identify different intellectual styles within it. What is more interesting and important, though, is the notion that there is not just one way of understanding and thinking about the activity of learning. Just as there are probably as many interpretations of the word 'mother' as there are people in the world (because we all have a highly personalized and unique relationship with our own mother – even within the same family or when she has been absent), so there are many competing ways to interpret the word 'learning'. As it would be impossible to document each of the different ways of thinking about learning, all we can really do is to look for areas of commonality – where different interpretations meet and coincide – that give us an insight into the various ways of thinking about learning. Both ideas – the preferred learning style and the personal construct of learning – are what inform your ways of working as a learner and therefore it is worth spending some time working out what they are. In the previous chapter we noticed how your learning preference can influence your study plan. Now we will look at the ways in which what we might call the 'personal intelligences' can have an impact on the ways in which you work.

Personal intelligence style

As stated in the first chapter, we live in a world in which the celebration of youth seems all pervading and this means that it is sometimes easy to forget that we gain an enormous amount of knowledge simply by living our lives and that this knowledge would never have been available to us as younger people. Many of the things we learn through progressing through life are what might be described as tacit knowledge – in other words, we rarely explicitly refer to what we have learned and we may have difficulty in putting it into words. That does not diminish the importance and significance of this type of knowledge, though, and it is often the sort of knowledge that helps us to survive. It is the sort of knowledge that used to be known quite simply as wisdom. Wisdom is a term that is less frequently used these days but the idea is still a strong one – that certain knowledge, which only life can give you is something that is far too frequently overlooked in books about learning. Increasingly research evidence from the field of health psychology suggests that our ability to resist breakdowns and mental illness is due to a sense of coherence – the way that we are able to draw together disparate aspects of our lives. It is personal intelligence – what Gardner (1999) calls the interpersonal, intrapersonal and existential intelligences allow you to create this coherence.

We all have different strengths and weaknesses. You will know from your own life that in some situations you feel completely useless whereas in others you will know exactly what to do and are able to take charge of a situation immediately. The same will be true of your friends and family and the situations will be very different from the ones in which you either excel or fail dismally. One of the benefits of ageing is that we build up a whole library and resource bank in our heads of how to deal with what life throws at us. We are able to use this information to varying degrees and we are stronger in some situations than in others. The reasons for this are manifold. Partly it is to do with our natural bias and the way our particular brain works; partly it is to do with the experiences to which we have been exposed; partly it is to do with the way that we have chosen to interpret those experiences and to make meaning from them. You have enormous strength and native intelligence that helps you to survive day to day. It is worth reminding yourself of this when you feel particularly anxious about your learning.

What is your approach to study?

As we discovered previously, the notion of learning is not universal or homogenous – it does not mean the same thing to everybody who uses the word to describe what they do. In the same way the processes involved in studying are very different according to different people. This section will help you identify what sort of a knowledge worker you are. A number of thinkers about learning styles have argued that because people process information in particular ways, this is linked to preferred ways of working in the classroom (see Further Reading at the end of Chapter 2). Kolb (1984) argued that people fall into one of the following categories – accommodators, divergers, assimilators and convergers – and that these suggested particular strengths in ways of working and possible career directions. The next assessment exercise will help to point you in the direction of your own preferred study style. Once you have established how you prefer to access and process information and also how that relates to the wisdom you have developed over a number of years and how you see the world, you can then begin to think about the way in which you work when you are studying.

The questions in the exercise that follows all relate to the way you work in academic and knowledge-rich situations. Your answers to these questions will give you your final analysis for this section: your study style. As with the other assessment activities in this book the point is not to encourage you to restrict yourself only to the activities that suit your style, but rather to make you aware of situations in which you may need extra support.

Study Style Assessment

Answer A, B, C or D to each question

1   Which of the following study situations would be the most enjoyable for you? Choose one:
A   A traditional lecture in which you take notes.
B   A group learning situation in which you learn by doing (for example, constructing a piece of equipment).
C   Reading secondary sources about whatever it is that you are learning and figuring it out for yourself (e.g. textbooks with diagrams etc.).
D   Working alongside an expert in a one-to-one situation for a while until you are able to pick it up for yourself and carry on independently.

2   What sort of learning situation do you find the most difficult?
A   Having to find out about something where you are completely in the dark and have no touchstones about who are the key thinkers or where to go for

(Continued)

(Continued)

information. A completely blank sheet without direction or structure is the situation posing most difficulty; for example, a completely open-ended assignment such as 'find out about post-modernism' without any direction.

B   Sitting in lengthy lectures delivered to large numbers of people with no opportunities to ask questions and no interaction, the expectation being that you will sit passively, taking notes.

C   Anything that involves strict supervision and over-reliance on group work, such as a strictly set out project which you have to work on with a group of colleagues on 'fun' active learning activities.

D   Any sort of completely bookish learning where you are left entirely to your own devices and where there is nobody that you trust or look up to as an expert to cast an eye over what you are doing.

3   How do you work on home-based tasks?

A   You draw up a schedule and keep to it – giving yourself breaks where appropriate. You prefer to work on your own without distractions.

B   You set yourself tests and tasks and you are a big fan of the dummy exam paper.

C   You cast your knowledge net very wide and use any number of sources to help you to understand a subject – including the internet and the media.

D   You work closely with the teacher's guidelines – basing your understanding of your progress on their comments on your work and even volunteering to do extra work in areas where you need practice.

4   How do you respond to assessment?

A   You put a lot of work into the task and you have a fairly good idea of what it is worth in terms of the assessment criteria.

B   It is more important to you to think about whether or not an activity is worth doing for its own sake than the assessment you get on your performance in the short term.

C   You work very hard on the things that interest you. You certainly feel a great sense of injustice when effort is not rewarded but you do have your own sense of a piece of work's intrinsic worth.

D   You are very reliant on the teacher's judgement for you to understand the worth of a piece of work. You accept what a good teacher tells you completely and you get a lot of satisfaction out of working in that way.

5   What impact do your peers have on your learning?

A   I enjoy their company as long as they are committed to the work.

B   They are essential – I enjoy solving problems as a team.

C   I like them as people but to be honest I prefer to work alone.

D   I am happy to learn with a small number of trusted friends who also work well with the teacher.

(Continued)

(Continued)

Analysis of Your Results

Mostly As – the classic student

You thoroughly enjoy traditional classrooms where expert teachers teach in a didactic way at the front of the classroom and you take notes, with time put aside afterwards for you to review your learning on your own and to consolidate understanding. You do not object to writing essays and you see doing examinations as a necessary evil in life. You are most at home when listening to an authority on a subject.

Mostly Bs – the engineer

You may not actually be an engineer but the term is useful because it demonstrates the hands-on, learning through doing, nature of your study style. You thrive on situations where a good deal of support comes through working with the group and you love the fun and competition of team work. You see very little point in doing anything if it does not have an ultimate purpose and you are extremely wary of the pursuit of knowledge for its own sake.

Mostly Cs – the monastic scholar

You are a self-directed enthusiast. You love working on your own and you see the pursuit of knowledge as an adventure. You see your teachers more as signposts than authority figures, preferring to regard the main bulk of the responsibility for learning as entirely your own. You may even be largely self-taught – you learnt at a young age that the best way of really getting to grips with a subject is to teach it to yourself.

Mostly Ds – the apprentice

Your strength is your ability to learn from others in a structured environment. A little like the engineer, you like to put knowledge into action but you are more reflective than that group and less dismissive of knowledge for its own sake. Theory goes hand-in-hand with practice for you and you gain as much from a detailed, useful conversation about a subject as you do from doing it. The one thing that influences you most, however, is your trust in your teacher. More than any of the other types, it is of vital importance to you that you can look up to and respect your teachers. When you strike gold with a good teacher you find that you really hit it off, and in the end they often find that they learn as much from you as you do from them.

Further Reading

- There is plenty of work available on the various types of learning styles. Richard Riding and Stephen Rayner's book *Cognitive Styles and Learning Strategies: Understanding Style Differences in Learning and Behaviour* (London: David Fulton, 1998) is a useful guide to the various theories available. Although much of the work is directed at children in schools, you may well find a lot of helpful information for yourself as an adult learner.

- If you would like to find out more about the notion of wisdom in human development you may find *Spiritual Intelligence: The Ultimate Intelligence* by Danah Zohar and Ian Marshall (London: Bloomsbury, 2000) a useful source of information.

- Honey, P. and Mumford, A., *The Manual of Learning Styles* (Maidenhead: Peter Honey, 1986) is an interesting read if you want to find out about another model of how individual learning style can have an effect on behaviour and study.

- Bernice McCarthy is also an important theorist in this area. She argues that there are four types of learners: innovative learners, analytic learners, common sense learners and dynamic learners. To find out more have a look at Bernice McCarthy and Dennis McCarthy *Teaching Around the 4MAT cycle: Designing Instruction for Diverse Learners with Diverse Learning Styles* (London: Sage, 2006). It is also worth looking at David Kolb's work the *Learning Style Inventory* (Boston, MA: McBer, 1978/1983). Also see Entwistle, N.J., *Styles of Learning and Teaching* (London: David Fulton, 1988).

- The work of Howard Gardner was mentioned in Chapter 2, but his work is central to many of the ideas presented here. In his 1999 work *Intelligence Reframed: Multiple Intelligences for the 21st Century* (New York: Basic Books) he updates his original list of seven intelligences from *Frames of Mind* (1993) and considers the evidence for three new candidate intelligences (naturalistic intelligence, spiritual intelligence and existential intelligence) and jokingly concludes that in fact there are eight and a half intelligences.

4 Confidence and Personality

This chapter will:

- Help you to understand which basic personality type describes you
- Link the work on learner and study types to an understanding of personality type
- Explore the connections between learning and emotions
- Introduce the idea of resilience and help you to understand how you can develop the skills needed to become a resilient learner

One of the biggest – possibly the biggest – problems facing you as an adult learner is your own misgivings about what you are about to do. This can range from the mild ('I don't know how I'm going to fit all of this in') to a severe lack of confidence ('I really have no right to do this and I shouldn't be here at all'). In order to help you explore some of the reasons for your lack of confidence and to help you find ways to overcome your misgivings, we really need to begin by asking ourselves what constitutes a thought and then exploring the sorts of thoughts we have on a daily basis which influence the ways we feel and the ways is which we act.

Who are you and how do you feel?

This may seem like a stupid question but it taps into something very profound about the way we operate as humans. Figure 4.1 demonstrates the links between thoughts, feelings and behaviour. Cognitive therapy teaches us that the ways that we feel, think and act are all inter-related and that we are in a constantly dynamic relationship with our environment.

As you can see, the thoughts drive the feelings which in turn inform behaviours. The behaviour stimulates a particular set of physical reactions which provoke subsequent thoughts. None of this happens in a vacuum. Your behaviour as an individual both influences and is influenced by the characteristics of both the learning and the wider environment. The classic example is the panic attack in which the person begins by feeling the concomitants of anxiety – perhaps palpitations and light-headedness – and this leads him to think that he might be having a heart attack. The thought turns

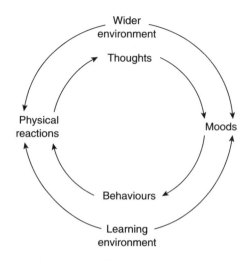

Figure 4.1   Links between thoughts, feelings and behaviours

his mood into one of panic and he responds by trying desperately to get out of the situation in which he is feeling so anxious. The panic increases his heart rate and makes his breathing more shallow and so his fears about the heart attack increase. Before he knows it he is in the middle of a full-blown panic attack. The startled reactions of people around him make him even more anxious, and so the cycle continues. There is hope though and cognitive behaviour therapists demonstrate how it is possible to replace the cycle with a more benign version by altering thought and behaviour patterns. Another way of deconstructing our reactions is to break them down into our feelings, which stem from our thoughts, which are provoked by the assumptions that we have about the world and these assumptions emanate from our deeply held beliefs (Figure 4.2). By identifying these beliefs we can analyse and challenge unhelpful ones.

We all have a number of beliefs about the way that the world operates and our place in it. Some of these beliefs are helpful and necessary ('I believe that I am safe in the company of strangers', for example, is vital if travelling on the bus is part of our daily working routine), whereas some are destructive if they are left unchallenged ('I'll never be any good at anything to do with study' is a pernicious idea for anybody attempting to learn). If we are able to recognize negative beliefs for exactly what they are, then we would realize that they are faulty, challenge and finally dismiss them. A belief can only be recognized as such by dismantling the structures that support it. Until we do that then the belief will continue to present itself to us as the only way of looking at the world. The problem is that most of the time we do not operate with any level of recognition of the nature of our beliefs. Instead we simply see the world as though our thoughts are true and given and therefore not to be questioned. As beliefs are often so embedded in our thought processes and actions, it is incredibly difficult for us even to identify what they are. For this reason it is useful to think about the feelings provoked by certain situations (such as when you are anxious) and then track back the thoughts

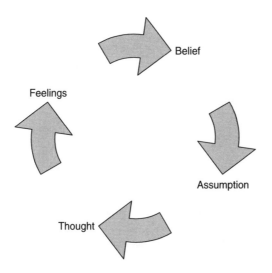

Figure 4.2   The cyclical relationship between beliefs and feelings

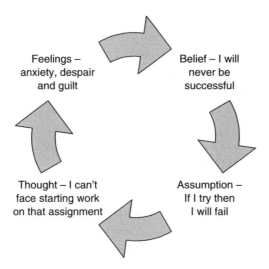

Figure 4.3   The cycle for an unconfident learner

that might provoke, the assumptions on which those thoughts are based, and finally the belief that drives all three.

In this way, a cycle for an unconfident adult learner may look something like Figure 4.3. You can notice the way that the core belief – I will never be successful – is a powerful driver for all the subsequent assumptions, thoughts and feelings. All too often the belief remains so concealed by those thoughts and assumptions that it is almost impossible to find it. But by challenging the thoughts we can begin to trace back the assumptions from whence they came and the beliefs that are driving them. When you notice an automatic negative thought ask yourself what are the assumptions and beliefs that are giving rise to it.

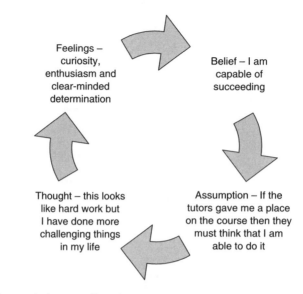

Figure 4.4   The cycle for a resilient learner

You will also notice that the faulty core belief – I will never be successful, or in other words 'I have not got the brain power to work at this level' – is like an incredibly strong engine, driving all the other elements of the cycle in a way that leaves the adult student feeling completely out of control.

By contrast, the cycle in Figure 4.4 shows the way that a resilient learner might think.

Challenging faulty beliefs

The first thing to say about a crisis of confidence ('I will never be successful') is that it is absolutely normal and a crucial part of the learning process. If the learning does not challenge you then it is not worth doing, but along with challenge goes the fairly significant phase of anxiety, which all learners go through. You could describe this phase as 'conscious incompetence' because it is this point in your learning that you begin to realize quite how much you don't understand and how much there is to learn. There really is no easy answer to dealing with this uncertainty – you have to weather the storm but, at the same time, knowing that anxiety is a common response for new learners will help you deal with it more effectively. It is a time to hang in there and also to be kind to yourself. To a certain extent, all transitions involve a certain amount of anxiety – it is an unavoidable part of life – but a return to learning brings back all sorts of memories of earlier educational experiences and some of these may not be very conducive to a feeling of self-confidence about learning. Learning also involves, to a certain extent, a reassessment of our identities. If you have always thought of yourself as a worker or parent or carer, it comes as something of a challenge to begin to see yourself in a new light – as a learner.

Learning means from moving from a position of not knowing how much there is to know (unconscious incompetence) to a realization of how much there is that we do not know (conscious incompetence) through to a situation where we know more than we realize (unconscious competence) and finally to a full knowledge of what we know and that we know as much as we need (conscious competence).

$$UI \rightarrow CI \rightarrow UC \rightarrow CC$$

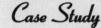

Case Study

Charles's story

Before starting a degree in education Charles was very confident about his views on how to make a child behave. Unaware of the research into behaviour problems and children's special needs, he thought he knew the answer to how to make children behave and he was baffled because the teaching profession seemed to be making such a bad job of it. He knew very little about the topic but was not bothered by his lack of knowledge because he was unaware of what there was to know. He was in a state of unconscious incompetence (or UI). After beginning his degree, though, Charles soon became aware of the challenges facing teachers in the classroom and the enormous amount of litigation, research and professional knowledge that informed their judgements. As such, he became acutely aware of how little he really knew (conscious incompetence or CI). Struggling with his lack of knowledge, he worked hard to make up for the shortfall by reading, writing and observations in the workplace. Before he knew it he was amassing a large amount of knowledge and understanding about behaviour in the school but he could not yet articulate that knowledge confidently (unconscious competence or UC). He still felt abashed by his previous ill-informed confidence. Finally, after researching and writing a 4,000 word assignment on a particular aspect of behaviour management in schools (the management of children with autism) he could feel fairly confident about his understanding of this topic and could talk about it lucidly because he had achieved conscious competence (or CC) in a particular area.

end of case study

The interesting thing to note is that Charles's pattern of self-esteem did not follow his increasing competence exactly. At the point when Charles was making the most progress in his knowledge – when he achieved unconscious competence – he was feeling worst about how little he knew. By understanding that there will always be this lag when your self-esteem and happiness about what you are learning struggle to catch up with what you have learned will help you to prepare yourself for the inevitable low that comes when you hit the UC stage of the process.

Other reasons for a lack of confidence are less to do with the learning itself and more to do with the people around you and their vested interest in keeping you where you are with your identity as a non-learner firmly intact. Ask yourself why these people don't want you to develop and reflect on any negative comments in this light. Developing self belief is the most challenging and complex of all the things you need to do as an adult learner. It is the most difficult of all the tasks facing you because it involves changing your identity. This Chapter will help you to find new ways of thinking about yourself in order for this to happen. It will also help you to answer the inner voice that says you are not up to it.

How do you see yourself?

We are all very different and that makes our experiences of learning very different as well. It is helpful to think about people in two categories – the eminent psychologist Dorothy Rowe calls these the 'what I have achieved today people' (introverts) and the 'people people' (extraverts). She explains in a range of her books, such as *The Successful Self* (1993), that introverts and extraverts often do the same things but for very different reasons. I have adapted her ideas to help you to explore your own motives for the way that you act. A sophisticated technique known as laddering is used by personal construct psychologists to ascertain whether somebody is an introvert or extravert. As laddering depends on highly individualized interchanges between questioner and questioned, it is difficult to represent in a book like this. The self-assessment that follows offers a rather crude representation of the differences between the two ways of seeing the world and is designed to prompt you to think about your own disposition. Some of the questions will make you think that your answer should be 'a bit of both'. This is perfectly natural but try to choose the one that most closely fits your gut feeling about what you would do. There are neither wrong nor right answers here, so don't try to choose the option that you think you ought to.

Introvert or Extravert?

Answer A or B to each question

1 Which of the following statements best describes your reasons for wanting to study?
A I want to move on and do something with my life.
B I am ready for a change and I want to meet some new people.

(Continued)

(Continued)

2   What do you want to get out of your studies?

A   I want to achieve something.

B   I want either a new group of friends or the confidence to keep up with my existing group of friends.

3   Which of the following statements most accurately describes how you feel about the course?

A   This is a big opportunity for me to do something with my life and I don't want to blow it.

B   I won't be able to fit into the group and they'll reject me.

4   What is the best thing about the course?

A   Knowing that I am getting somewhere at last.

B   The good laugh that we have in the sessions.

5   When you lose confidence in your ability with your learning, what does it feel like? Try to think about how it felt to attempt to do something that you really needed to learn but were unable to.

A   I can't keep on top of this work – I'm losing it and it's all falling to pieces.

B   I am totally lost in all this work – I can't remember why I started it and I don't even know who I am any more.

6   How do you respond to criticism?

A   I am ok if it is someone I don't rate – then I can ignore it – but if it is from someone whose opinion I value I go to pieces.

B   I am ok if the criticism is given in a kind way – I can take any amount of criticism if the person is warm and friendly and helps me move on. It is when the criticism is accompanied by rejection that I panic.

7   How do you feel if another student asks for your help?

A   Proud – my ability must be clear to someone! As long as it doesn't get in my way I'd be happy to help.

B   Really pleased and happy to help – I like being helpful to people.

8   When everything is going to plan and you are enjoying the writing/presenting/reading, which of the following statements best describes how you feel?

(Continued)

(Continued)

A   I love creating order from all the chaos – all the messy notes from lectures and the scribbles in margins of the books I have read coming together in a coherent assignment makes me feel really pleased.

B   I love making free connections when I get going with an assignment. I love finding out what one person thinks and what the other one thinks and being able to find out what the consensus on an issue is. Then I like talking to all the people I work with and thinking about how the ideas relate to my own life and the people I know.

9   What are the most difficult situations for you when studying?

A   When the information is coming to me from all sides and when the goal posts keep on changing. When the pressures keep interfering with the schedule I have set myself. Then if I start missing deadlines I feel like I am failing and the whole thing feels like it is slipping out of control.

B   When I am on my own looking at books that seem to be completely abstract to me and not in any way connected to my real life and my own priorities, then I feel completely out of my depth within the group – they all seem so much more confident and clever than I am. If they find out just how little I know they will all reject me and I'll be thrown off the course.

Count how many answers you have in As and Bs

Analysis of Your Results

The **A** answers are **introvert** responses – you are a 'what have I done today?' learner. This means that you tend to define yourself in terms of what you are able to achieve and the clarity that you can bring to the world around you. The **B** answers are **extravert** – you are a 'people person' learner. This means that you tend to define yourself in terms of the relationships that you have with other people and you take great pleasure from being part of a group.

These results will begin to give you some idea of what makes you tick. Now you need to play on these strengths and find ways of working with your weaknesses. The main thing to understand about the introvert/extravert theory is that people in

(Continued)

(Continued)

each category do the same things but for different reasons. So either an introvert or an extravert may stay up all night to finish a presentation for the course she is doing but the motivation will be very different. For the introvert it will be very important to establish a sense of something done well – to achieve. She may also be negatively motivated by the fear of the whole presentation going to pieces in front of the group and of her looking and feeling as if she is out of control. For the extravert acting in the same way the motivation will be very different. For her the main motivation will be to contribute something useful and real to the group of learners. She may also be negatively motivated by the anxiety that she will be rejected by the group if she does not come up to scratch and meet the standard set by her peers. As you can see, therefore, it is far too simplistic to state that extraverts and introverts act in completely different ways. Most of the time we act in the same way but for completely different reasons. It is facile to simply assume that because somebody is very confident in a crowd and appears to be sociable at a party, that they are an extravert. There are plenty of introverts around who have learned the necessary social skills to operate in these ways. They may have learned them the hard way, though, and made a lot of mistakes along the way, unlike their extravert friends who may well have these skills naturally but for whom the struggle up the career ladder, for example, may have been much more of a challenge.

Case Study

Heather – mostly As

Heather is an achievement-orientated learner. She is studying for a foundation degree in the arts. Knowing she is an achievement-orientated learner has helped her to manage her studies over the past two years. She knows that she is at her best when she is working to a structure so she has devised a system whereby she plans her life on a monthly basis, allowing for her children etc., and writes her study times into her diary at the beginning of the month. She is very rigid about keeping to her timetable once she has done it. She knows it would not suit everyone but so far it is working for her. She needs to ensure that her need for control does not overwhelm her and to learn to let go every so often.

end of case study

Case Study

Alan – mostly Bs

Alan is a people person – his learning is at its most effective when he is able to build relationships with other people. He is currently studying for a foundation degree in education. He loves going to the college sessions and having fun with the group and he often feels that he is making some useful contributions. At first, though, when he got home, he found that his mind went blank and that all the fun and liveliness of the sessions just disappeared. He has developed a way of annotating the texts with notes about real situations and people he works with. For example, when reading about how leaders cultivate a learning environment he underlines it and he writes in the margin 'Jan (deputy head) was really keen for me to do this course and encourages me to talk about what I am learning to the other LSAs'. In this way he has helped to make the less real (the abstract theoretical concepts) real by directly connecting them with things from his own working context. In addition to this technique he has used his naturally extravert personality to galvanize other members of the group who live locally to meet in a pub once a month to talk about progress and to catch up with the members of the group.

end of case study

The strengths and weaknesses of each type of learner are given below.

Introverts (achievement-orientated learners)

Strengths:

- Can work alone happily

- Work well with deadlines and structures

- Able to voice contrasting opinions and get debate going

- Obsessive nature means learners can immerse themselves into a subject

- Perfectionist tendencies mean that a very high standard of work can be produced.

Weaknesses:

- Perfectionist tendencies can cause stress and make learners miss deadlines because the work is 'not right'

- Can take criticism badly and fall to pieces as a consequence

- Can be inflexible in unpredictable circumstances

- Can find working in groups very difficult

- Hate not being in control – not good in new and unfamiliar situations.

Extraverts (relationship-orientated learners)

Strengths:

- Work well in groups

- Enjoy lively debate and can bring a lot of fun to learning situations

- Able to make the connections between life and theory well

- Turn learning into action very well

- Excellent at presentations and teamwork.

Weaknesses:

- Can feel lonely and isolated when working alone

- Can put popularity above correctness and this may hamper confidence about expressing original, individual thoughts

- Can let deadlines slip by getting caught up in the flow of day-to-day activities

- Can be bothered by the abstractness of some concepts and ideas

- Can allow the need to be liked to dominate decisions about what to say in class and assignments.

If you are an achievement-orientated learner then your priority should be to control the things that you can and learn to relax about the things that you can't. If you are a relationship-orientated learner then you should find ways of integrating contact with others into your learning.

Negative and positive emotional states

The thoughts that accompany distinct negative emotional states tend to cluster around certain common areas. Depressive, hopeless states are characterized by the thought that life and learning has no meaning, for example. The thoughts associated with anxiety generally surround the thought that we are in immediate or imminent danger, that we are threatened by something (such as failure) or someone, and that we are ultimately vulnerable in some way or other. The thoughts often predict the future and this tends to be an unmitigated catastrophe. Of course, catastrophes and tragedies do frequently occur but they are not always the outcome. An important part of managing anxious responses to study is repeatedly to ask yourself, 'what is the worst thing that can happen?'

There is no doubt that negative emotions can interfere with your learning. Feeling positive emotions, on the other hand, can have the reverse effect. The doctor, Alice Domar, has done a good deal of research into the effects of relaxation on the body and mind (Domar and Dreher, 1996). She argues that there is a definite, tangible effect of relaxation on the brain. In the same way that the fight or flight response has a certain physiological impact on brain chemistry and the immune system, so the identifiable relaxation response, which can be achieved through twenty minutes of mind–body relaxation techniques such as yoga – can have a measurable and identifiably beneficial impact on the body and brain.

The meaning of study and learning

It is important just to consider for a moment what study means for you. We often take for granted that we all have a common understanding of the same ideas. For example, we assume that everybody knows what jealousy or love feels like. But as we saw in Chapter 3, there are as many different interpretations of the words and concepts as there are people. As somebody who has chosen to work in education for years and who enjoys learning and studying for its own sake, my concept of learning is that it is an exciting, enjoyable and peaceful activity that can also be frustrating and very hard work. I go into academic and professional learning activities with the expectation that I will enjoy them. I have a clear understanding what study means for me and although I know that study is often intellectually stimulating and challenging and I know that real progress comes when we are able to take ourselves out of our comfort zones, I do not have any particularly negative expectations of study. I have noticed over the years, though, that this concept of study is a long way from the construct of study that many students have. It has taken me a long time to realize that some people not only have an expectation that learning has to be a terribly serious hard slog but also that if they are enjoying themselves then something must be wrong. It is very difficult to reason with such students. I have seen them steadily and methodically burn themselves out by their perfectionist drive to get everything right and to leave no stone unturned. This is particularly true of many students on professional learning courses, such as teacher education. Faced with the enormity of the task (learning how to become a teacher, for example), many people retreat into their own academic pursuits, trying to control what they think is more controllable than the real life complications of the professional workplace. 'Take it easy and be kind to yourself' the tutors say, seeing that the student has become so entrenched in particular ways of thinking and so glued to his books that he cannot see the wood for trees. Typically the student responds politely, showing appreciation for the concern, but then goes straight back to the old ways, muttering to himself that the tutor must have very low standards and expressing surprise that such a person could get to a position in life where they are arbitrating other people's learning. Within the first term, typically, the student will have missed deadlines and sometimes interrupted his studies or dropped out altogether. What such students fail to understand is that the really big breakthroughs in learning come not when we are chained to the books or the computer for 10 hours a day but in the playful gaps between periods of study. It is absolutely essential that you recognize that there is a very important place for fun and enjoyment in the learning process and to change your concept of study to incorporate it, if necessary.

Fun and learning – laughter is good for you

Just as the relaxation response can have major benefits in terms of our mental and physical health, so fun and laughter can help enormously in the learning process. We discovered in the previous section that it is important for us to think about what studying means for us and to be prepared to change our views and constructs if we are to learn most effectively. In the same way that some people resist the notion that learning should be difficult (it should be challenging or you will never progress), other people never allow for the fact that learning can be enjoyable. It is important to understand that not only is it helpful if learning is fun (because it means that you are more likely to stick to it) but it actually makes the learning more permanent.

Optimistic and pessimistic approaches to learning

We have all heard of the saying that you are either the type of person who sees the glass half full or the glass half empty. We sometimes mistakenly get the impression that this is a genetic disposition about which you can do nothing. This is really a long way from the truth. By challenging your core beliefs as a learner you can begin to question some of the things you say and the thoughts that you have. This is not a luxury; it is absolutely necessary that you adopt an optimistic view of yourself as a learner if you are to succeed. Try to move yourself from a pessimistic approach to learning to one of optimism. As a guide, optimists tend to see failure as temporary, reversible and that it could happen to anyone (for example, 'this particular essay has failed but I can soon put it right with the advice of my tutor and his advice will be helpful when I go on to do all the subsequent work for the course'), whereas the pessimist will see the negative response to learning as fixed, immutable and personal (for example, 'I have failed this essay and this clearly shows that I am not up to the standard needed for the course and therefore I never will be. I had better drop out now.'). Adopting an optimistic approach to learning and life has enormous benefits for our long-term physical and mental health. Sensible optimism is a good way to explain negative events to yourself. As we established previously, thoughts determine feelings, so if you can alter the way that you think to a more optimistic approach then more relaxed feelings will follow. Look again at the diagram about the resilient learner (Figure 4.4) and notice how the learner's thoughts and behaviour feed back into the beliefs she has about herself. Here are some practical ways that you can challenge your own thoughts and behaviours to reflect a more optimistic approach to learning.

Developing a more assertive and optimistic approach to learning

Try to swap the examples of things that a pessimistic learner might say, on the left, with things that an optimistic learner might say, on the right.

Pessimistic learner	Optimistic learner
I shouldn't be here	I am glad that I have been given this opportunity to show what I am capable of
Everybody else seems so much more confident and intelligent than I am	Some people talk a lot when they get nervous. I am one of those people who need time to settle in and understand a situation
If I say anything at all I will look like an idiot	I'll risk an opinion because the environment is perfectly safe – the worst thing that will happen is that I will be corrected
I'll never be able to manage to write 3,000 words	3,000 words seems like a lot but I have faced plenty of other challenges in my life and succeeded

They all make me feel so old and incompetent	I'm so glad that I'm not in my early twenties anymore. I had forgotten about how much other people's opinions matter at that time. Life has taught me a lot that I did not know at that age

Pessimism black spots

Just like ice on a road is dangerous but not lethal if you know where it is and so how to avoid it, so it is worth knowing in advance when the challenges to your confidence will most likely come. In general we feel the worst when something attacks one of our core beliefs. This causes us to lose confidence and feel bleak about ourselves and the future. So, if your mind always went completely blank in examinations at school, causing you to fail the examination, you may have developed the core belief that you will always fail an examination. So if you then fail an examination as an adult learner it will hit you much more ferociously than if you had always put your success or failure down to luck in the past. By identifying the negative beliefs you can begin to anticipate the knocks to your confidence and take aversive action. Here are some common examples. The core belief is presented in the middle column in bold italic.

Event causing knock to confidence	*Beliefs tapped into*	*Alternative way of thinking about it*
Presentation to the group goes wrong	They are all laughing at me – they think I am an idiot. *I always make a fool of myself when I speak in public*.	That was bad luck – I either didn't prepare well enough or I misread the task – I'll learn from the experience.
You are not invited along for coffee with the other members of the group	They don't like me – I don't fit in. *I never get on well with my peer group*.	They probably didn't notice me sitting there – I haven't said much yet. I'll go over anyway. I know that it takes me a bit longer than other people to make friends but when I do I have very good friendships.
An assignment fails	I'm not up to doing this course – they have now found out and will ask me to leave. *I am not very bright*.	I have been accepted onto the course so I will trust the professional judgements of the tutors – if they think that I can do it then I can do it.

A tutor is unfriendly and ignores you	She doesn't like me, I can tell. *I never get on with authority figures*.	She probably is so absorbed in what she is doing that she didn't notice me. If she doesn't like me then so what – I'll survive.
A tutor makes a fool of you in front of the rest of the group	He made them all laugh at me. *I'll never fit in with a classroom situation*.	I'll speak to him at the end of the session to let him know that my feelings have been hurt by the way he spoke to me. Then I'll make a note never to treat anyone else like that.
Work commitments mean that you have to miss a deadline	I'm in trouble now – they will think that I am lazy. *Now I have fallen behind it will all fall apart*.	So I have missed one deadline. It was unavoidable but I will soon be back on track.

Managing the negative messages

There is no point in underestimating the difficulty of changing your self-image. It has taken a long time to develop your core beliefs about yourself as a learner. They will have developed as a result of environmental factors, past and present, and the way that you have decided to process these factors and to make meaning from the world. Early on we make meaning from events in the way that will best help us to survive but these core beliefs cease to be useful when our lives and environments change. A core belief is only revealed as such when you cease to think that it is the only logical way of looking at a situation and begin to understand that it is one of many options. The challenge is, therefore, how to get at your core beliefs. By using the ideas from the cycle in Figure 4.4, you can begin to track your thoughts and feelings throughout the day. It is a good idea to use an automated thought chart to record your thoughts at troublesome times – such as times of pessimism or anxiety. An example is given below. It has been adapted from Greenberger and Padesky's useful book *Mind Over Mood* (1995).

The highlighted thought is what is known as the 'hot' thought because it is driving all the others. Your challenge is first to identify the hot thoughts and then to provide for yourself alternative ways of thinking.

Situation	Feelings (score each thought by the percentage that it is experienced)	Automatic thoughts (images)
Preparing to write the first 3,000 word assignment – browsing in the library trying to find books that will help	Anxiety (60%) Confusion (15%) Worry (15%) Embarrassment (10%)	I don't know what I'm doing here I don't know where to find the books on this list Everyone will see that I have no idea what I am doing The essay will fail anyway I'm not up to doing this course Maybe I could back out now

Other people

As soon as you have started on the course of tracking your own unhelpful thoughts you will begin to notice how many negative ways of thinking are identifiable and prevalent in the people you know. Some of these will relate to you and your learning but you will also notice that they will tap into core beliefs about their own inadequacy. Dealing with other people's negativity is as much about protecting yourself from their anxiety as it is about asserting your own needs and rights. So try not to get into the situation where you are propping up other anxious or depressed students – your own confidence needs to develop rapidly in the early stages of a course and anxiety can be very contagious. Try to be helpful, while at the same time developing boundaries.

Resilience and the adult learner

Looking after your emotional health in learning situations is an important aspect to the learning process. Try to understand where your vulnerabilities lie and how to anticipate them. In the same way get to know your own individual responses to those situations. Some of us will always respond with anxiety to difficult situations whereas for others a depressive response is more usual. It is helpful to think about your emotional health in the same way as you do your physical health. This means that it is important to take preventative actions. Some ideas for keeping you emotionally fit, healthy and resilient are offered below.

1 **Complexity is good**   Like a food chain in ecology, the more complex your life the more difficult it is to break down. Remember, though, complexity does not mean hassle – just the amount of different things going on in your life that define your day-to-day existence. This means that for the person with nothing more going on in his life than just his job, when the job goes wrong he is much more vulnerable to breakdown than someone for whom his job is just one of many facets of his life – including his family, friends, love of cooking Indian food, membership of the pub quiz team and his part-time degree in Philosophy. For this man, whose life is significantly more complex, if something goes wrong with his job then he has other support systems to fall back on. It is tempting when embarking on a course of study to think that because it is so time-consuming you must give up all other hobbies and social arrangements. This is entirely the wrong thing to do. It is important that you keep up with all the things that give your life meaning to help cushion the blows of learning. It is fine to re-appraise the time you spend on various activities but you should hold onto them as much as is possible.

2 **Give yourself rewards**   In order to build resilience it can be quite useful for you to adopt what is known as a behaviourist approach to learning. This will involve building in rewards for your own progress. The rewards need not always be linked to high-level performance. Try to add some in that are simply about getting through the course itself. Think about the assessment of your learning style preferences in the previous chapter. If you are a textual learner who finds yourself having to work in a predominantly pictorial mode for a while give yourself a reward for just doing it, regardless of the grade you achieve.

3 **Use humour**   A good sense of humour is one of the most effective things you have in your armoury against failure. Laughter is literally good for you – it promotes particular physiological changes that are healing and helps you to get the negative event, such as the failure of an assignment, into perspective. When things do go wrong – and they will – it is a good idea to imagine yourself telling the story of the problem (a failed assignment or making a fool of yourself in a seminar) to a trusted friend. Try to emphasize the funny aspects of it as you give the account.

4 **Avoid catastrophizing and try to keep a perspective**   Something that marks out people who are particularly prone to depressive and anxious responses (and hence a propensity to drop out of courses and to give into failure) is that they immediately jump to the worst case scenario in any given situation. This is known as 'catastrophizing' and it has a poisonous effect on your attempts to study because if you give into it you will allow the correction of mistakes to take on a far greater significance than they deserve. We learn by making mistakes and without them it is virtually impossible to move to the next level. In any situation that threatens to overwhelm you ask yourself two questions:

- How can I turn this situation into one in which I survive in a stronger position than I was before?

- What new knowledge is being offered to me here that is of value in the future?

Try to get into the habit of training yourself to keep things in perspective and focus on your ability to survive – you have got this far in life by being a survivor and there is no reason why you shouldn't get further.

Further Reading

- Dennis Greenberger and Christine Padesky's book *Mind Over Mood* is a very helpful text about how we can manage our responses to life events (New York: Guilford Press, 1995). Figure 4.1 has been adapted from one from the Center for Cognitive Therapy cited in *Mind Over Mood*. It comes from the tradition of cognitive behaviour therapy and deals mostly with anxiety and depressive states but the principles established are very useful in the management of less extreme emotions. The ideas about automatic thought tracking and the links between thoughts and feelings in this chapter have been adapted from that book and I would recommend it in particular if you have a lot of these negative thoughts.

- Dr Raj Persaud's book *Staying Sane: How to Make Your Mind Work for You* (London: Metro Books, 1997) has a wealth of information about how you can build up your emotional defences as an adult and is a useful read for any adult embarking on a learning activity. His ideas about resilience and safeguarding one's emotional well-being in order to preserve mental health are groundbreaking and I recommend it if you are interested in the ideas relating to complexity and the avoidance of catastrophizing in this chapter. He argues that 'The mentally healthy person doesn't necessarily sail through their divorce, sacking or bereavement, but is less prone to nervous breakdown on such occasions... In other words mentally healthy people are able to learn emotionally from whatever life throws at them.'

- The conscious incompetence etc. model is used widely in management consultancy and training circles and is attributed variously to a number of theorists including Dubin, P., *Human Relations in Administration* (Englewood Cliffs, NJ: Prentice Hall, 1962), but its origins may go back much further. The model corresponds roughly to an anonymous oriental proverb:

  He who knows not, and knows not that he knows not, is a fool – shun him,
  He who knows not, and knows that he knows not is ignorant – teach him,
  He who knows, and knows not that he knows, is asleep – wake him,
  But he who knows, and knows that he knows, is a wise man – follow him.

- If you are interested in finding out more about the origins of the introversion/ extraversion categorization you should consider looking at Jung's original theory of personality types (Jung, C., *Psychological Types,* trans. R.F.C. Hull, *Collected Works of Carl Jung*, vol. 6, Bollingen Series XX, Princeton, NJ: Princeton University Press, 1977) and the way that the Myers Briggs personality profile adapts these ideas to a definitive test (see Myers Briggs, I. *The Myers Briggs Type Indicator Manual*, Princeton, NJ: Educational Testing Services, 1962).

- Finally, if the work on personal construct theory (see the section in this chapter about how you 'construct' study and learning) interests you then an accessible introduction to George Kelly's ideas is Butt, T. and Burr, V. *Invitation to Personal Construct Psychology*, (2nd edn) (London and Philadelphia: Whurr, 2004). If you are ready for the original text then George Kelly's 1955 text, *The Psychology of Personal Constructs*, vols 1 and 2 (New York: W.W. Norton) is the book for you.

5 The Physical Aspects of Learning

This chapter will:

- Examine the mind/body connection
- Explore the findings of research on how the food we eat and the lifestyle we lead can have an impact on the way we work and learn
- Discuss how the space and place in which we work can help or hinder the learning process
- Look at how ICT can contribute to this understanding of the physical aspects of learning

We have become accustomed to thinking about the mind and body as two completely separate entities. The division of the various specialists in the medical profession reflects this way of thinking – psychiatrists and psychologists work with people's minds and surgeons work with people's bodies. This is actually a relatively recent construct and it reflects a way of looking at ourselves that is particular to a Western 'scientific' way. Throughout history people would have been much more likely to regard themselves in a more integrated way – seeing the whole self as being in a state of illness or wellness. It is helpful to think in this way when we embark on learning because how you feel and how well you are can have a profound impact on the way that you learn; equally, the states of anxiety and elation that are sometimes provoked by learning can, in turn, affect your health.

The body clock

We all know that we are more effective at different times of the day. Anybody who has ever done a presentation or had to chair a meeting after lunch knows why the hour between two and three o' clock in the afternoon is commonly known as the graveyard slot – because everybody is so sleepy that gaining a reaction from your audience is extremely difficult. We also know that people who work shifts that are constantly changing are more likely to make mistakes and have accidents than those who work a more regulated, rhythmical pattern. Most of us also have a fairly good understanding of how much sleep we need – some of us can get a way with very little and still perform well (Margaret Thatcher famously existed on 4 hours a night) and others of us really need 9 hours in order to feel alert for the following day. The National Sleep Foundation (www.sleepfoundation.org) recommends that adults need an average of 7–9 hours of sleep a night and some studies show that the average adult is operating on significant sleep deprivation at any time. Much of our understanding of the way we work at different times of the day, however, is highly dependent on the culture and climate of the country in which we live. The Spanish spend less time asleep at night but take a siesta after lunch – returning to work in the late afternoon and evening. In Britain and North America we divide our days up much more rigidly – taking all our rest in one block and working through an 8-hour-plus day in one go.

Tiredness

Many of us feel tired a lot of the time. To a certain extent this is for very good reasons – modern working hours are long and arduous and this factor alone is often enough to make us feel tired. Coupled with other pressures – the demands of a baby or a very elderly relative in the house, for example – it is no wonder that constant tiredness is a way of life for a lot of people. I am not seeking to pretend that these problems are easily surmountable – they are the very real conditions which make up the realities of modern living. There are many things that we can do, however, to make sure that we are not feeling more tired than we need to be feeling. We can take more exercise, for example, avoid foods that 'burn up' very quickly and leave us feeling tired and hungry after a very short time and we can work with, rather than against, our own natural body clocks. It is well known that the brain does not operate effectively when we feel tired. We have all had the experience of being unable to remember an important fact – a name or a telephone number that we have used thousands of times in the past – when we are feeling particularly tired or stressed. At times of running on empty the brain will seek to protect itself by selecting the functions that it considers to be the most important. The problem for us as adult learners is that we may not agree with its selection! When we experience stress for a really prolonged period we are in danger of experiencing burnout altogether, so, it is very important that we attempt to combat tiredness wherever we can.

Fighting against evolution

Our place in history has a big influence on how we see time. In industrialized, economically rich Western countries we tend to labour under the illusion that time is defined by the framework that we have invented. As a society we have lost touch with the way that daylight and the weather determine our activities because technology and science have conned us into believing that we can override nature. So we can pop out at 2 o'clock in the morning for a loaf of bread and a tin of beans because the supermarket is open 24 hours a day and we don't need to worry about the cold, dark winter nights curtailing our activities because our cars are heated and electric lighting makes most things possible, however dark it is outside. It is only when we are hit by a spell of extreme weather, such as snow, that everything grinds to a halt. This clearly has brought us great advantages as a society but it is also very problematic. We have forgotten our roots, and many of us now live lives that we did not evolve to live as a species. We have taken thousands of years to reach this state but the changes that technology and industrialization have wrought on our lives have only really happened in the past 150 years. This means that our brains have not caught up with our all-weather, 24/7 lifestyles. No wonder we have trouble concentrating at certain times of the day.

There are three things that we can do to make sure that our minds are in a good, alert condition for study: we can make sure that our diet includes a variety of nutrients; we can make sure that we take sufficient exercise; and we can make sure that we get enough daylight. In fact, high intensity light can have a huge impact on mental health – a one-hour walk in the daylight can have a major benefit on our minds and our potential to learn best.

The point is that for our ancestors much of the productive work would have to be done in the warm, light summer months in preparation for the winter when all activities would necessarily be curtailed. Without electricity it would be impossible to keep working (whatever that work was) into the late or even mid-evening because there would be no light to see by. Deep winter would likewise be a time for preserving energies and keeping safe – there simply could be no expectation that people would work as hard in the winter as in the summer because there was no way that they could. We shouldn't be surprised, therefore, that we feel so tired and lethargic in January and we certainly shouldn't persecute ourselves for the fact. Rather, we should respect our evolutionary traits and try to work with the way that we naturally work, rather than fighting against it. As with most things in life, you can be most effective if you work with nature rather than against it.

Owls and larks

Most of us have an inkling about whether we are a morning (lark) or an evening (owl) person. We know that we are more tired in the mornings or in the evenings. For each of us the cortisol hormone peaks at different times of the day. This means that some people are intellectually alert and physically energetic in the mornings and for others the reverse is true. The following exercise will help you to clarify your understanding of when you work most effectively.

Owl or Lark?

Answer A or B to each question

1 It is your birthday. If you had a completely free rein and did not need to take any of your friends' wishes or practical requirements into account and you had to choose one of the following options, how would you prefer to celebrate it?
A A dinner party.
B A lunch party.

2 You have an assignment to finish or an examination to revise for and time is short. What do you do?
A Stay up until the early hours to finish the work.
B Go to bed at the normal time but set the alarm to get up very early to finish the work.

3 How much can you eat in the mornings?
A Very little – I can't face food until mid morning.
B As much as I have time for – I usually have a good breakfast.

4 If you had to give a presentation at work or as part of your course, which would you prefer it to be?
A Later in the day.
B Earlier in the day.

5 If you had no commitments or disturbances and could arrange your day entirely to suit your own moods and rhythms, what time would you prefer to get up (choose the time nearest to the one you would prefer)?
A 10.15am
B 6.45am

6 You decide with a friend to embark on a new exercise regime. You can find one hour in each day that you can both commit to. Which would you prefer it to be?
A 9.00–10.00pm
B 7.30–8.30am
Count how many answers you have in As and Bs

As you will have guessed, the **A** answers all describe **owls** and the **B** answers all describe **larks**. There is a continuum between the two which encompasses extreme Owls who feel so negative in the mornings that it verges on a depressive state but who can party into the night quite happily, and Larks who are sharp and alert first thing in the morning but feel so tired at the end of the day that a late night party literally makes them feel tired for days afterwards. Most of us, though, are somewhere in the middle with moderate tendencies towards one or the other end of the continuum. It is worth noting that the old adage, attributed to Benjamin Franklin, 'early to bed and early to rise makes a man healthy, wealthy and wise' and so clearly favours larks, seems to have no truth in it. So owls need not feel badly about their score. Catherine Gale and Christopher Martyn showed (1998) that there is no evidence that larks are luckier than owls in terms of their cognitive performance or health.

You might want to check to see if your result is correct by performing the same sort of task (perhaps making notes from a text that you are using for your studies) at different times in the day over several days, making a note of how easy you found it to concentrate and how much or little time it took you to do the same amount of work. The later in the day that you performed the task in a short time span with good concentration should point you further towards the owl end of the spectrum. Do try to avoid the post-lunch graveyard slot, though, when all of us perform less well, regardless of our overall time preference. Keep a diary to record when you work best by choosing a sample day once a week for the period of about a month. This will help you to avoid choosing an atypical week (such as one where you had several broken nights sleep) and getting an unreliable result.

Once you have decided whether you are an owl or a lark use it to your advantage. Your mind will always be much clearer and your thinking sharper in your preferred time of the day. Once you have got used to working within your generally preferred time of the day try to narrow it down to an even more subtle understanding of timings – if evening then what sort of time in the evening is best for you? If you enjoy working in the mornings the most, then how early is best for you to start? The stress hormones cortisol and adrenaline are said to be higher in the morning but at what point in the morning will depend on your own particular body clock. By combining this knowledge with an understanding of the effects of food on the body you can really begin to refine your ways of working so that you can work at optimum strength most of the time.

You can use daylight to boost your levels of alertness when you need them most. For example, if you are an owl you should try to get outside in the daylight as early in the day as possible – even if it means going outside into your garden while you wait for the kettle to boil. If you are a lark, try to incorporate a late afternoon spell in the light because this will give the message to your brain that it is still daytime and help you to avoid that slow but steady shutting down that makes you so sleepy in the evenings. Your preference for mornings or evenings is also a good indicator of when it will be best for you to exercise, by the way. Larks will always do better when they exercise earlier in the day and early evening exercise will always be more productive for owls.

Time and timetables

When you first start studying after a time out of the classroom it is tempting to think that you need to set yourself a timetable which is similar to a working day – i.e. 8 hours per day. You will quickly find, though, that this only has a certain amount to offer the adult learner because learning happens in fits and starts. You will find that at some points you are flying ahead while at others you feel that you are making no progress at all. Most projects and writing activities involve quite a lot of ground-laying work. This is laborious and tiring. At this stage it can be very difficult to motivate yourself to work quickly and effectively. Once this is done, though, it is a common experience to find that as you near the end of the project and just as time is running out you suddenly become completely absorbed in the task and are able to sustain long periods of concentrated work. 'If only I had worked at this pace at the beginning of the project' we wail. But this is precisely the point. The work is only able to gather its own momentum when you have done all the groundwork – you could not have worked with the degree of urgency and enthusiasm at the beginning of the project because at that stage you had no material knowledge to work with.

Some people find that marking the time spent studying in hours and minutes is the best way to chart progress. If this works for you then it may be worth setting up a time sheet in the way that you would if you were doing some contract work. Write down the time you start each session of work and when you finish and remember to allow yourself breaks. Try to suggest to yourself that you will do a minimum of work per day. The advantages of this system are that it allows you to keep a tally of how much you do and it will suit you if you are a person who needs tight discipline within which to work.

An alternative way of monitoring how much you work is to measure what you achieve rather than how long it takes you to do. Depending on the task you could measure the amount of words you write or the number of questions that you answer for example. Set yourself a target – perhaps of writing 500 words per session – and make this a minimum target, regardless of how long it takes you to do. This method has that inbuilt incentive for you to finish the work as soon as possible. If you finish the work quickly then the rest of the day/evening or weekend is your own to do what you like with it. You will need to build in time to review the quality of the work if you decide to organize your study periods entirely by timescales. Finally, you might want to use reverse psychology to motivate yourself to get the work done. Instead of saying that working for 3 hours or writing 500 words is your minimum, you might want to make it your maximum. So by saying that you will not *allow* yourself to write more than 500 words or that you will not work for more than 3 hours you make yourself regard the work as a treat rather than a chore.

Emotions and learning

Now that we have established that there are two basic personality types that influence learning style we can begin to have a more detailed look at the way that emotions can influence learning.

The effects of the emotions on learning are profound. We talk a lot about stress and its effects on the way we feel but what is often underestimated is the profound effect those periods of sustained anxiety (which is many people's response to an external stressful situation) can have on our mental and physical health. Just as pertinently it can have a serious impact on the way that we make decisions and take in and respond to information. We have already established that effective learning occurs when we feel secure. This is dependent on two things: your external surroundings and interaction, and your own internal thought processes. Ensuring that both are ok is actually quite a challenge. Although there is much that we can do to minimize the amount of stress-causing situations to which we are exposed, no amount of careful planning can minimize them all. In fact, by attempting to control these external factors we expose ourselves to possibly the most damaging form of stress of all – the futile attempt to control what is beyond us. The only thing we really have any true control over is our own emotional response to situations. So how do we minimize the effect of pernicious emotions and prevent them from blocking our true potential as learners?

Fear and anxiety

It is well known that the 'fight or flight' response is produced when we are placed in anxiety-producing situations. The body responds by releasing hormones into the bloodstream that allow us to work beyond our normal physical capabilities and either run away (flight) or face the cause of the anxiety (fight). The rapid response team of hormones result in a heightened sense of physical and mental arousal. There are ways of reversing the effects of this stress on the body and mind and we will look at these in the next chapter. It is worth pausing here, first, to consider the long-term effect of living our lives in this way.

Physical effects of prolonged anxiety

The miraculously beneficial effects of the stress response in small doses become destructive and dangerous in the long term. There are two ways in which this can happen. The first is the direct effect of those hormones and chemicals that are produced by the stress response on the rest of the body. The second is the behaviour that commonly follows from stress and that is also dangerous in the medium term. Activities in this category include drinking excessively, smoking, taking recreational drugs, over- and under-eating and becoming sleep-deprived. As far as the body is concerned these effects of the direct chemical onslaught include: hypertension and chest pains, heart-burn and indigestion, abdominal pain and feelings of rapid and constant tiredness. The medical links between these conditions and long-term serious conditions such as cardiovascular disease and some cancers continue to be established.

The effects of stress on the brain

The physiological effects of stress included an impaired reaction time, disturbed concentration and poor physical coordination. You will know that you are experiencing stress by the presence of some or all of the following:

- **Increased irritability**

- **Heightened sensitivity to criticism**

- **Loss of concentration**

- **You dwell on the worst possible outcome – that the assignment will fail and that you will be thrown off the course**

- **You become obsessive about just one subject – such as getting the assignment finished above all other considerations**

- **Pounding heart and palpitations**

- **Sweating**

- **Feeling sick and dizziness.**

None of this is good news for intensive study. Worry, fear and anxiety all take our minds off the task in hand – these emotions suck us into a vortex of self-absorbed anxiety and we have to learn to train our minds not to give into the pull away from the subject in hand. In short, we have to learn how to distract ourselves and study is a great way to do this. As such, the studying can be an enormous help when we are going through a difficult patch. Many of the most successful adult learners have told me over the years how important it was for them to continue with their learning at precisely the moment when it was most difficult to do so. There is gathering evidence that we are more likely to have accidents when we are under stress (common sense would tell us that this is the case anyway). An evolutionary theory of why this happens might be that judgement of a situation is blocked in situations where there is a prolonged anxiety response. This might be the ego trying to protect itself from something that is severely disturbing. In the modern world, though, the result is likely to be one of misjudgement. Hence the familiar feeling of being so stressed that we cannot think straight. On the other hand, some individuals who are particularly anxiety-ridden in examination situations may divert up to half of their cognitive powers on time-wasting activities such as 'feeling' nervous and blaming themselves for not having revised etc. Ironically at precisely the time when such people need all of their mental powers, only half of them are available.

Fighting the 'fight or flight' response

As we established in the previous chapter, stress has a big impact on the body and mind. It is well known that when we feel what is commonly known as 'stress' it is due to the 'fight or flight' response that has its basis very early on in the evolution of the human race. The links between excess adrenaline – a sure sign that the individual is experiencing stress – and serious diseases such as coronorary disease and cancer are beginning to be established. The evidence continues to grow that stress also has a major part to play in other conditions such as infertility and irritable bowel syndrome (IBS). We all know tacitly that it also has a major part to play in the way that our brain functions and the way that we feel about ourselves and life. There is a difference between acute stress – such as the stress that is set off if we are attacked, for example – and chronic stress, which develops incrementally as we face the challenges of real life day-by-day. The first type of stress is usually easy to recover from – providing it does not happen too regularly. This type of stress is actually very useful if you are going into an examination or about to do a presentation. It is the second type of stress that really takes its toll, though. It causes us to live in a constant state of mental and physical hyper-responsiveness – we all know that state where we live at such a level of stress that we feel just one little thing will completely send us over the edge. One of the main parts of our brain to malfunction when under stress is memory. This is because the brain goes into emergency drive and filters out everything other than information that is directly relevant to dealing with the cause of the stressful situation. Clearly, then, it makes sense to remove as many of the negative stressors as possible from the learning environment.

Dealing with stress and fatigue

Breathing

Science has recently begun to agree with some of the ancient traditions that have been used over thousands of years to teach the human race how to deal better with their bodies, minds and the world around us. Yoga is one such discipline that we can all use to get the best out of our mind and body and which will allow us to think about things differently.

The word yoga means 'oneness' and is often meant in the broadest sense of being part of something. Devotees of yoga resist the arbitrary mind – body separation that has dominated Western thinking for the past two centuries, instead regarding the mind and body as integral to the whole self and not in any way separate. As well as the most well-known aspect of yoga – the postures or asanas – meditation and breathing form important parts of the discipline. Both have much to teach us.

According to the yogic principles, we tend to breathe in a very shallow, inefficient way that runs counter to the way that we have evolved to breathe. As Julie Page, a British Wheel of Yoga qualified yoga teacher, explained to me, 'if you watch your dog resting you will notice his abdomen rising and falling steadily with the intake of breath. This is also what should happen when we breathe. We tend not to do this, though, instead directing the breath towards the upper chest and rib cage rather than the belly. In yoga we argue that this compromises our potential and leads to an ever-present feeling of tiredness because the lungs never fill completely with sufficient oxygen and waste products are never completely expelled from the lungs'. In your pursuit of effective learning you could do a lot worse than signing up for a course with a good yoga teacher, but even if you do not want to go that far you might want to try to concentrate on simply breathing more slowly and deeply whenever you can. This will slowly become a habit. The practice is also an excellent way to counteract stress and anxiety.

Quietening the busy mind

We tend to think of the skills involved in learning as emanating from the rational brain – the comprehension, analysis, synthesis and evaluation required to really understand a topic all come from the same brain functions: reasoning and language processing. It is important to remember that this is only a small function of the whole mind, though. The mind is capable of operating on much deeper and higher levels and it is worth your while to get to grips with other ways of working with the mind if you are really to get the best out of it.

In modern, Western societies such as the UK and the United States we tend to believe mistakenly that we *are* our thoughts. Instead of our thoughts being products of our mind – which is much closer the mark – we allow ourselves to become so involved in responding to the thought itself that we do not give ourselves chance to dismiss it or to question it. Meditation, which has a long and fascinating history in world religions and philosophy, can give us sufficient distance from our thoughts to simply watch them pass across our minds like clouds in the sky. As soon as we have achieved this distance from our thoughts we can begin to filter out those thoughts that are useful and choose to ignore those that are not. You can then (after the meditation, not as part of it) begin to subject thoughts to the sort of analysis we discussed in Chapter 4. The benefits of meditation are manifold for you as a person – it has been proved to lower blood pressure and improve the immune response, for example. For you as a learner, however, there are very specific benefits. These are:

- **It allows you to experience an 'empty', mind – free from the constant noise of thoughts about past and future.**

- **It rests your mind and body in a way that is deeper, almost, than any other experience, thus improving your mental agility and ability to concentrate when you apply your rational thinking to a study task.**

- **Some of the deepest insights and important understandings can emerge at the end of a meditation. You will go back to your learning with a renewed vigour and perception.**

- **Practising meditation allows you effectively to get more hours in the day. As you become more practised in meditative practice you will begin to notice that you need less sleep. This is because the quality of relaxation is so deep that the mind and body no longer need extra sleep to find rest.**

There are many approaches to meditation and there are plenty of good books on the topic. At first it is a good idea to find a quiet place where you will not be disturbed to do your practice. When you have become more skilled you will find that you will be able to meditate anywhere – in fact it is the best portable tranquillizer available! It is a useful way of calming yourself before an examination or interview. In the beginning, though, you will need to find the right environment in which to work. Sit with your eyes softly focused on your object of meditation and breathe slowly and deeply. Once the meditation starts you can breathe normally but you may find that some breath focus work (such as the abdominal breathing described earlier on) is helpful to help you relax. Try to increase the time that you spend meditating gradually, just aiming for a couple of minutes at first before building up to 10, 20 and beyond, depending on how much time you have available. At first you will find that every manner of thought crowds into your head and it will be a struggle not to be distracted. Do not worry about this. Simply watch each thought as it arises but do not fight with it or follow it. Here are a couple of techniques that may appeal to you.

A *visual meditation*

A well-known, simple meditation is to focus on a candle flame burning. Try to absorb the picture of the flame completely, notice the shapes it makes and the colours that make up the light. After some time, close your eyes and now reproduce the picture of the flame in the space between your eyebrows. Now 'watch' the flame for as long as you can, breathing normally as you do so.

A mantra meditation

Another popular meditation method is gently to repeat a word or phrase, either out loud or in your mind, again and again. The choice of word is up to you – if you have a faith you may want to choose an inspiring phrase or word from a spiritual text. Alternatively you might want to focus on the state that you aspire to – such as repeating the word 'calm' on the in breath and 'peace' on the out breath. Experiment with a few different phrases before you find the one that suits you.

You may be interested in putting your understanding of meditation in a stronger philosophical or spiritual framework. His Holiness the Dalai Lama expresses this idea perfectly:

> Buddhism explains that our normal state of mind is such that our thoughts and emotions are wild and unruly, and since we lack the mental discipline needed to tame them, we are powerless to control them. As a result, they control us. And thoughts and emotions, in their turn, tend to be controlled by our negative impulses rather than our positive ones. We need to reverse this cycle, so that our thoughts and emotions are freed from their subservience to negative impulses, and so we ourselves, as individuals, gain control of our own minds. (HH the Dalai Lama 2000: 6)

Exercise

We established at the beginning of the chapter that it is helpful to think about the body and the mind as being not only connected but as one organic whole – the person as a whole being. Given that, it is too simplistic to talk about how exercising the body can help the mind to work more effectively – you will be benefiting your whole self if you can refresh yourself by walking around the block and by getting more fresh air. Exercise has a powerful effect on your mood as well as your ability to concentrate and perform cognitive tasks. It has a marked anti-depressant effect on the mind due to the production of the body's own painkillers and energizing hormones. So it helps to remove the stress that can block learning. It also acts as a good way of distracting the mind from unhelpful loops and giving you a new perspective on whatever it is that you are learning about. Studies show that exercise – even very gentle exercise – can have an enormous effect on your mood – making you feel happier and more relaxed. As we have stated all the way through this book, learning is an emotional as well as a cognitive activity that is very much influenced by our mood and level of general well-being. There is also evidence that light has a beneficial effect on our mental health and well-being and, if this is combined with exercise, there is a double bonus for our mental agility.

Fresh air

Studies have shown that decision-making skills and mental agility are sharper after exercise than before and that long-term exercise can lead to improvements overall. Scientists are not quite sure why this is, but some argue that increased blood flow (and therefore oxygen) to the brain is the reason for the benefits. Humans have an instinctive desire to feel part of the natural world (although this may be hidden) – it is the way that we were designed and have evolved. By getting outside for some fresh air – by walking or in a wheelchair – we can enhance the emotional benefits of exercise. If possible try to choose a form of exercise that is good for your mind and soul as well as your body. You will go back to your studying invigorated and with a clear mind. Don't punish yourself for this time spent outside away from your books – often our most important insights come from the times when we are resting or relaxing. Nietzsche said that all truly great thoughts are conceived by walking and it is good to bear this in mind when we are tempted to tell ourselves that time away from books and the computer is wasted time. The thinking process goes on whether we are aware of it or not. By allowing yourself substantial times of rest and contemplation you will find that the quality of your thinking improves overall.

Diet

We have already established that if you try to work without being in the right mindset or if your body is too tired to allow you to think clearly, then you are more likely to fail than if you have an understanding of your mind and body working together in synergy. In the same way, there is a very clear link between the way you treat your body (in terms of what you feed it and how much exercise you give it) and the potential that your mind has for working effectively.

Here are a few facts that are worth bearing in mind as you make decisions about what to eat in order to get the best out of your brain.

- **Excess starch leads to the production of serotonin in the brain and this can make us feel more drowsy, sluggish and in need of a nap. When you are feeling very anxious and that everything is getting on top of you, a meal of starchy carbohydrates (including most of the things that we tend to think of as comfort foods – white pasta, mashed potatoes and bagels) can be just what you need. Most of the time while studying, though, you will be after the opposite effect – to make yourself more alert and engaged. By eating a meal based on protein, fruit and vegetables, you can keep your energy levels steadier.**

- **Protein creates feelings of fullness after a meal – so we tend not to eat quite so much if we include protein in our diet. It also means that the substance** dopamine is stimulated in the brain. This makes us feel more alert and helps us to concentrate more and feel less sluggish.

- If you are feeling tired the right combination of protein and carbohydrates can do a good deal to make you feel more alert – try to choose fruit over sweets, though, to prevent your insulin levels from surging uncontrollably and making you feel more hungry again.

- Make sure that your diet includes a range of nutrients. In particular try to incorporate sufficient vitamin C combined with iron in your diet to help you to avoid anaemia, which can cause poor concentration and confusion – not ideal conditions for study!

- Vitamin B1 (found in pork, eggs, grains and cereals) is also useful for boosting concentration and clarity. The B vitamins in general are important, as are folic acid and selenium. Oily fish are said to be particularly good for promoting mental agility and health.

Water

We tend to be rather dismissive of things in life that are free – preferring to invest our money and energies in things that the advertisers persuade us to think are the miracle cures for everything. Water is free (if you drink the tap variety) and plentiful and it has an enormous amount to offer the learner. Some researchers argue that 30–40 per cent of us are in a state of dehydration most of the time. There are plenty of physical effects of this lack of water – fat cannot be broken down as efficiently, for example, there are also proven effects of dehydration on the brain. The advice from the British dietetic association is to drink five pints a day – three as straight water and two in the form of water-packed fruit and vegetables. Water plays an important function in helping us to feel less tired; we often reach for a sugary snack when, in fact, all we needed to do was drink a glass of water. Dehydration also dulls your mental function – not good news for studying.

Caffeine and alcohol

Caffeine often gets a bad press, not unjustifiably so, it has to be said. We know that in large amounts it is certainly addictive (many of us will have experienced that awful withdrawal headache if we have deliberately or inadvertently gone without our usual tea or coffee for a day) and it can lead to palpitations, anxiety and insomnia when drunk in large amounts. As an adult learner, though, you can use it judiciously to your advantage. It is a mood elevator and can certainly make you sharper. As all students know as well, there is nothing quite like it to enable you to burn the candle at both ends on the odd occasions when you have to finish a piece of coursework for a deadline or to cram in some last minute revision for an examination.

British doctors recommend that a healthy intake of alcohol consists of no more than 14 units of alcohol for women and no more than 21 units of alcohol for men, and that these units should be spread throughout the week and not stored up for the weekend! Although the debate about the benefits of alcohol continues, it is well to remember that there is no nutritional value in alcohol and that any benefits relate only to the consumption of small amounts. The effects of alcohol on the brain are well known – most of us have experienced the fuzzy feeling that is enormously relaxing at the end of a hard week when we have a glass or two of wine. Of course it goes without saying, this is not a state that is conducive to learning and studying – that is the whole point of using alcohol to relax – it helps us to switch off. It is also worth bearing in mind that alcohol has a significant dehydrating effect and so all the negative effects of dehydration on the brain are multiplied when we consume alcohol. The main point here is perfectly obvious – the glass of wine with your partner or friends, while being a wonderfully relaxing start to the evening in normal circumstances, will wreck your study time if you intend to read or write in the late evening. Also, if you are planning to spend a whole day studying on a Saturday, try not to have more than three units the night before or the hangover will interfere with your best efforts. Once you have handed in the coursework or completed the examination, of course, there is nothing to stop you from celebrating with a few drinks!

The reason that both alcohol and caffeine are habit-forming is partly because too many of us use them as the only ways we know to quickly alter our moods. Rather than concentrating on the process of cutting down on the amounts that we drink of both substances, it might be more beneficial to develop the repertoire of methods available to us that can help us to change our moods. These include exercise (as discussed earlier), listening to music and altering our thought patterns (as we looked at in Chapter 4).

Space and place

The environment in which you work can have an enormous impact on the quality and enjoyment of the learning experience. In an ideal world we would all have a book-lined study to work in, but few of us are lucky enough to have access to such a room. Instead, most of us use our spaces to multi-task – we clear away the debris to find a path to the table and then we have to clear away our notes and computer because it is time to eat – regardless of what delicate stage we have got to with our writing. Some of us find that despite all our attempts to find a quiet, peaceful place in which to work, our homes are never sufficiently conducive to intellectual endeavour and instead we seek the peace of a public space such as the municipal library or university computer room.

There is a danger of getting a bit too hung up on the search for a quiet space in which to work – kidding ourselves that if only we could find that elusive space then we would be able to work alone for hours. Let's not forget that Chekhov apparently wrote most of his important plays and short stories at the end of a kitchen table in a noisy, busy family household. There is no denying, though, that we are ultimately affected by the environment in which we work. So if at all possible, try to negotiate time when you will be left alone by friends and family members. If necessary, take the telephone off the hook and try not to respond to the strategies that others may use in order to distract you. Here are some practical tips about how to make the most of where you find yourself working:

- If you have to, use earplugs, and not just for the home environment – public libraries are not the strictly policed temples to learning that they used to be. You could use a traditional personal stereo headset with the CD/tape function turned off if you feel uncomfortable with cotton wool in your ears.

- Try to have all the books and texts that you will need for a session around you from the start. If you have to keep getting up to find books you will easily become distracted.

- If you are working on the computer, switch off the on-line facility. If this is not possible then resist the temptation to check your e-mail while working. Not only is it a waste of time but it gets you into a practical, superficial level of thinking that is not conducive to thinking deeply about your work.

- Property is nine-tenths of the law! The more that you can claim the space for your study, the more people will respect this and expect you to use it . This also goes for university and public libraries. People will expect you to be in a regular spot at the weekends and find themselves somewhere else to sit.

- If ear plugs do not work for you and you prefer background noise that is not distracting then choosing a type of music that is not your usual preference can be very enlightening. Classical music for the rock fan and jazz for the classical buff can work wonders because you will not 'tune in' to it in the same way that you would if you were interested in it. The main thing is to choose a non-speaking sound source.

- Don't underestimate the importance of posture and correct typing technique. Check that you are sitting up straight and that you are not straining any part of your body when writing. (This may sound like boring advice but you will really regret it if an injury means that you are unable to continue with your work at a crucial stage.) It is worth noting that the majority of people who use a computer to write have not been trained as typists. The techniques that secretaries use to

negotiate the QWERTY keyboard are well established and have been developed for a purpose. If you intend to do a good deal of your work on the computer and have never been trained to use it, it might be worth your while to spend some time working on a typing software program. This will also help you to speed up your work.

Setting up your study

Although the body can sustain work in a variety of conditions and psychological tests have shown that carrying out mentally demanding tasks is not generally adversely affected in hot conditions (as long as the temperature is not so high that it affects the body in other ways), we all know that an inhospitable temperature – whether too hot or too cold – can interfere with our ability to do our work effectively. Few of us are lucky enough to live in a house that allows us to have our own working environment with all the ideal conditions, but a brief appraisal of what is needed may give you some ideas for how you might adapt your current arrangements.

As much use as possible should be made of natural light but it is always worthwhile investing in a good desk lamp that casts a light directly over your work, rather shadowing you from it. Computer work demands a lower level of background lighting than general working conditions because the computer screen generates its own light. As far as levels are concerned the keyboard is usually best placed slightly lower than a table and the monitor slightly higher. If at all possible try to find a unit that incorporates various height levels so that you can experiment with the best possible arrangements. Try to place the keyboard at a height and distance away from you that means that you do not need to hunch your shoulders or slump forwards in order to operate it effectively.

The ideal working environment would also include a large desk or table that would allow you to spread all your books and papers around your computer (if you are working with one) in such a way that all the information you need is readily available and you can cross-reference points immediately. Shelves are very useful in a study so that you are able to store work and texts to keep them out of other people's way and yet still up together and readily accessible. Much attention has been paid to e-Books (books presented in electronic form on the computer) in recent years but it has to be said that nothing can really beat the pure tangibility of the real book. We grew up learning to turn the pages and look at indexes and basically to read in a linear fashion. It is a good idea to make as much room for your books as possible, therefore. More and more people choose to work on a computer but of course it is still perfectly possible to operate without one. The main thing to remember about working on a computer is that you should bear in mind posture. Try to find a chair that supports your back and maintains good posture. The height of the PC in relation to your wrists and eye-level is crucial in determining the levels of comfort and avoidance of straining.

Silence and noise

We discussed in Chapter 4 that there are two types of people – introverts and extraverts and that the distinction is determined by the levels of stimulation in the brain. Extraverts tend to be able to tolerate, and indeed seek, a good deal more external stimulation than introverts. Think about this when you make the decision whether or not you want to involve background noise. Some people say that they cannot work without a certain amount of background noise whereas it is an anathema to others. Of course it goes without saying that if you are in a public space – such as a college or public library – you should assume that others want to work in silence.

ICT

If you are lucky enough to own a laptop (notebook) computer it can help enormously with your work as long as you have worked out an effective way of working on the computer. The only problem with the laptop is that if it is used in the way it has been designed – literally to sit on your lap as you work – it is notoriously bad for the posture when used for long pieces of writing. It really is worth finding a table of an appropriate height to work on instead. Few of us these days have received direct teaching in touch typing, which is worrying as most of us spend a good deal of time typing on computer and there are significant possibilities of repetitive strain injury because of this. It is well worth taking advice on how to sit at the computer and making good use of things like hand rests.

It is worth remembering to save your writing in a variety of places – electronically and physically – when you are working on lengthy pieces of work. Back up your files using discs at different stages of your work and make sure that you store them in a separate place from your computer (so that if the computer breaks down or your laptop is stolen you do not lose the back-up versions as well). In the later stages of the work when the prospect of losing all that you have done becomes really scary it is even worth keeping a printed version of your work in another location again. If the worse comes to the very worst then you will have something to scan and you will not be left without anything. The computer breakdown is the twenty-first century version of 'the dog ate my homework' excuse and tutors have heard it all before! You may be surprised by the lack of sympathy you receive when you tell them about the fiasco that has led to the non-appearance of your assignment. It really is your responsibility to manage the technology with which you are working and to have back-up plans when it fails.

Using the Internet

We are living in an age of information overload. Arguably there is more access to information than there has ever been. The problem with information on the Web is that it is rather difficult to judge the authority of the websites and the origins of the information included in them. The best way to judge the authority of the work on the Internet is to go through reputable sites – such as the BBC online site – and to look for links for your chosen subject or to go through recognized academic sites such as Google Scholar and to restrict your search at first to refereed journals. The fact that a journal is refereed means that the material in it has been deemed to be publishable by at least two other academics. This at least gives you some indication that the work is useful and reputable.

Plagiarism and passing off

Finally, a word about plagiarism. The Internet has opened up new ways that work can be copied. There are sites available where you can buy ready-made assignments and research that has already been done and then pass this off as your own. I cannot warn you away from these sites strongly enough. In practical terms, much of the work is of a very poor quality and is really not worth investing in – even if by some strange chance you are able to find a site that deals explicitly with the exact subject that you are wanting to look at. Secondly, in my experience universities and colleges are now taking this sort of thing extremely seriously and employing the strongest possible sanctions against students who take work from the Internet. Most universities have plagiarism panels and they now know the extent to which plagiarism goes on and are hyper-vigilant about the practice. Avoid it – the consequences may be dire if you don't.

Further Reading

- The market is awash with books on diet, but for a book that deals explicitly with the links between food and the brain you might like to look at David Benton's *Food for Thought: How What You Eat Affects Your Mood, Memory and Thinking* (London: Penguin, 1996).

- The relaxation response is dealt with in detail by Alice D. Domar and Henry Dreher in their book *Healthy Mind, Healthy Woman* (New York: Henry Holt, 1996). Although this book deals with issues that mainly affect women's health men will find the generic sections on the science behind the theory of the relaxation response and ways you can elicit it very useful as well.

- Erica Brealey's book *The Spirit of Meditation* (London: Cassell Illustrated, 2004) is a beautifully presented argument for learning to meditate with plenty of ideas about how to do it. If you are interested in finding out more about meditation you will certainly find a method to suit you here.

- For more information about sleep and the owls and larks patterns of sleeping and waking you might want to look at www.bbc.co.uk and search for 'sleep'. The quiz in this section has been adapted from the one on this site. The Surrey Sleep Research Centre generates a good deal of work on sleep that you may find useful.

6 How Did You Get Here?

This chapter will:

- Help you to identify examples from your life where you have learned more and less effectively
- Explore how these situations have helped you to construct a particular view of yourself as a learner and to build up your understanding of what learning is
- Give you some guidelines for how to use this information to deal with situations you encounter as an adult learner

Whenever we encounter a new situation for the first time – be it going to a foreign country or starting a new course – we think of it as a novelty, a new thing. The human mind has not really evolved to deal with novelties, though. Instead, it prefers to process new information on the basis of old knowledge – we cope with the new situation in the way that is shaped by the way we have dealt with similar situations in the past. The problem is that as humans we don't perceive the contextual differences particularly well. We prefer to use a blueprint set down in the past, rather than construct a fresh understanding on the basis of something new: our minds tend to apply old rules to new situations. This is both a good and a bad thing. If we are kicked by a horse as a child we learn quickly not to hover around the back ends of ponies and we apply this rule for the rest of our childhood and into our adult lives, which is fine as long as we do not want to pursue a career as a farrier. If we fail dismally at French at school, though, we quickly learn that we have little aptitude for foreign languages. We avoid having to speak them if we can and if we are forced to do so we feel embarrassed and cowed.

The way that we revert to established patterns of behaviour is particularly true of situations that involve fear. Under pressure we short-circuit logical and considered ways of thinking and return to tried and tested survival techniques. It is similar to the way that when we are on holiday we can enjoy driving around the country lanes, taking time to enjoy the countryside views and not being too bothered about our time of arrival. On a Monday morning, however, or on the way to a job interview, we plough straight down the motorway at 70 miles per hour, even though we know that there could be hold-ups and that the volume of traffic is enormous. Under stress we take the most accessible and well-driven routes, even when we know that it might not be good for us to do so.

In terms of learning, this means that although we might consciously acknowledge that we are happy adults and that we have accomplished many things since we were children, our brains are still dealing with the world according to rules set down with our early experiences. This means that when we see our new tutor standing at the front of the class, we do not think 'here is a new person and I am open to being taught by her'. Instead we make judgements about her based on the last person we encountered in such a situation, and this was probably a secondary school teacher. Thus we act according to our experiences but the conscious mind does not necessarily know what games the unconscious mind is playing. It is really important that we acknowledge where our previous notions of ourselves as learners have come from because they will have a major impact on the way that we deal with the new situation as an adult.

In order to help you to see your previous learning experiences more clearly it is worth building up an educational life history. This will allow you to create what we shall call your learning autobiography.

Creating your learning autobiography

Stage 1

Think about two things that you have learned. They can be experiences that involved formal learning, such as studying maths at school, or informal learning, such as learning to ride a bike. One of the experiences should be something that you remember fondly – an example of learning that worked for you – where learning was **effective**. The other experience should be an example of when you remember your own performance as unsuccessful – where the learning was **ineffective**. You may remember this experience with frustration or even anger. So, for example, an experience of effective learning might be learning to swim (if that came easily to you) whilst an example of ineffective learning might be learning to drive (if that was something of a nightmare). Now, on a piece of paper write down all the possible reasons why your experiences were either good or bad. An example of how you might do this is given below.

Jane is in her early 40s and she remembers the two examples – learning to swim and learning to drive (see Figures 6.1 and 6.2).

As you will see, clearly the first example holds lots of positive memories for Jane: the atmosphere, teaching and built-in rewards helped her to be motivated and she was successful as a result. In the second example her poor relationship with her teachers and preconceived notion of her own lack of ability had a detrimental effect on Jane's learning. In the first example, the fact that the course took place in a happy, sunny place helped considerably. In the second example, the fact that Jane was finding the money to support her driving lessons from a meagre wage packet had a detrimental effect on the learning.

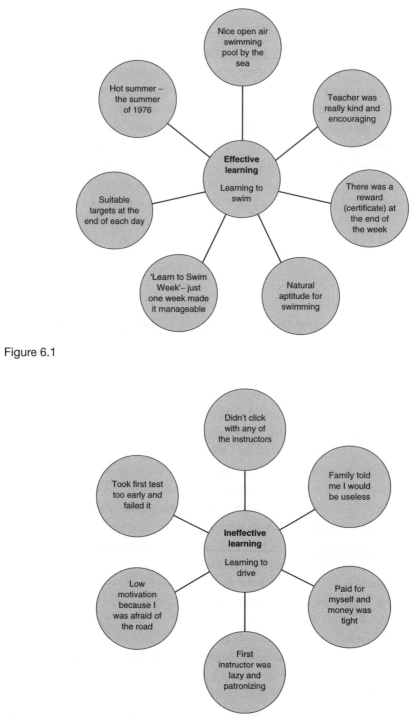

Figure 6.1

Figure 6.2

From these two brief examples certain themes can easily be spotted. They are:

- **conditions**

- **incentives**

- **pre-conceived notions of ability**

- **the learner's relationship with teachers.**

Conditions   There is an obvious contrast between the sunny weather and open air pool in which Jane learnt to swim and the cramped car in which she attemped to learn to drive. Not only was the former more pleasant and so conducive to effective learning but it was also free space in which Jane could develop with confidence. The driving instructor's car was, conversely, very much his territory rather than hers. It is important to recognize the impact of physical conditions when learning and to improve them where possible. Another group of conditions is emotional factors. For effective learning to take place the learner requires support and encouragement and they need to trust the course.

Incentives   In the first example the swimming was well structured in terms of achievable goals each day and a reward at the end of the week. The finale for the whole week was applause and celebration. In the second example the rewards were not attractive because Jane could not see a way to using the driving skills because she would not be able to afford a car at the end of all the driving lessons and she did not really want to drive – feeling safer on public transport. It is helpful if you can identify rewards and incentives for yourself throughout the course. Treat yourself to something as you complete each stage and tap into the notion of extrinsic motivation to help you work harder.

Ability   The main problem with Jane's attempts to learn to drive was that her efforts were constantly hindered by the messages that had already been given to her about her perceived lack of talent and coordination skills. These are powerful and totally destructive messages and the damage done by people who make such proclamations on the basis of poor information is massive. Remember the advice from Chapter 4: try to identify the core beliefs that are driving your thoughts and if they are unhelpful then dismantle them. Each time that you find a negative assumption behind a thought, challenge it.

Teachers   The relationship with the teachers is crucial in both examples. Jane remembers her swimming teacher 30 years later – clearly, as a kind and gifted teacher. Jane remembers her first driving instructor as 'lazy and patronizing' and although she does not elaborate, it is clear that he had little thought for her welfare. Like Jane, we all learn most effectively when we feel secure, supported and motivated and we learn less effectively in situations where we feel insecure or where we feel that the teacher does not have confidence in us.

You will probably have found your second example, that of ineffective learning, more difficult to write. This is because you will have negative associations with it and you will find it quite upsetting to think about. Key to making your future learning effective is recognizing that these associations are the blocks to your learning and finding ways to structure your future learning such that these impediments can be minimized. If you have a very negative response to a teacher try to de-personalize the situation and identify exactly what it is that he or she is doing to provoke such a negative response from you. Is it that the teacher is disorganized, teaching at too high a level for you or boring? When you have worked out what it is that is making you feel unhappy then try to talk to the teacher about the problem, but be very careful about how you voice your concerns. As with all discussions about conflict situations, try to focus on the action rather than the person who instigates that action. Instead of saying 'You are teaching at the wrong level', put the emphasis on *your response* and ask for help in dealing with it. So 'I seem to have developed an irrational anxious response when you ask us to work at higher levels. I wonder if you can help me with it,' will be much more likely to elicit a helpful, non-defensive response. People always respond better to requests for help rather than attack.

Personal construct psychology is a helpful theory in this context. Its founder, George Kelly, as Burr and Butt (2004) have shown, saw human beings in a state of psychological motion – we are always making meanings from the world around us and acting on those constructions of meaning. If you can understand the meaning that you are making of a particular learning situation then you can begin to appreciate that there may be alternative meanings to be made about that same situation. In other words, there are different ways of telling the same story. So, your tutor is not necessarily being rude to you because she thinks you are unworthy to be in the group, for example. Rather, she is just unhappy in that particular situation and is probably making her own meanings of it, regardless of what you are doing.

Stage 2

The list of questions below will help you to analyse your own learning history. This is the next step in creating your learning autobiography.

Prompt Questions on Learning History

Write a couple of sentences in answer to each question.

1 Try to remember something about an early learning experience – perhaps learning to read or how to do your times tables. What can you remember about the learning activity and your feelings about it? Was the learning effective or ineffective?

2 How did your parents or guardians influence your learning? Was formal learning taken seriously in your household? What were the rewards for success and how was failure dealt with?

3 How did your learning fit into the family set-up (interpret 'family' according to your particular circumstances)? Were you always the 'clever' one or was that characterization always given to your sister/brother? If you could go back in time to the age of 9 or 10, how would your parents/carers describe you as a learner/student?

4 What did your friends think about formal learning? Did you approach learning in the same way as your friends or did you stand out as different from them? How did you talk about homework/exams?

5 How might your teachers have described you as a learner? How would they describe your behaviour towards learning? What were your school reports like?

6 What learning have you taken as an adult? Have you learned new skills at work or as a parent? How easy was it for you to learn these new skills?

7 What are the two key lessons that life has taught you? (These are the things that you can't ever learn in a classroom – the things that only experience can teach you.) How did you learn these things?

Now look back over your answers. What general themes emerge? Are there links between the answers, or words and phrases that you have repeated several times? Use the ideas below to help you to interrogate your answers in more depth.

1 The important thing here is the nature of the experience that you have chosen as significant. It might be that this memory is quite familiar to you or it could be that something has occurred to you that you have not thought about for years. Your mind has selected something that fits into your own story – the narratives that we construct and tell about our lives.

2 Our parents and carers are a major influence on the way that we think about learning and ourselves as learners. If you grew up in an environment where learning was highly valued and where your achievements were praised and where you were supported through your difficulties, then you are likely to have a confident, positive approach to learning. Most of us, though, do not fall into this category.

We might grow up in households where learning is not valued and we are ridiculed for our mistakes. Or the environment may be intensely competitive, where study is the only thing that matters in life. In such environments all the joy of learning is destroyed in the face of grim competition. Our parents or carers only praise the most outstanding successes, condemning our mistakes and failures. The way that your parents/carers thought about learning in the past will have an impact on the way that we regard it now – even though they may not still be around to judge us.

3   It could be argued that all families and well-established groups (such as a stable team at work) ascribe rigid roles to their members. These roles almost work like scripts in a play and like actors on stage, if one actor decides to ad lib and to disregard the script then all the other actors panic and work hard to bring the delinquent actor back into the play. A similar thing happens in families – all members have a vested interest in making us stick to the script that has been written for us. This is the reason why, at big family gatherings like Christmas we often find ourselves falling back into old ways of acting. So instead of being the successful, independent person that we know ourselves to be, we become a sulky 17-year-old again on a very short fuse with our siblings. It is exactly the same with our sense of ourselves as learners. If your family has always cast you as the member of the family with lots of common sense but not much intellectual ability then it will be very easy for you to step back into that role. The challenge for all of us is to recognize that the role was created for us early in our lives and then to disregard it. If members of your family still find it difficult to cope with the idea that you will achieve something through study then simply be more circumspect about who you tell. Ration the time you spend with unsupportive people. It is your chance to shine now, so get rid of the old image of yourself that you have from years ago. It is inaccurate, out of date and it helps nobody other than the people who have a vested interest in keeping you where you were for the sake of boosting their own flagging self-esteem.

4   Schools are interesting, hierarchical places. Even in the most liberal comprehensives there is a strict pecking order set down by the teachers and pupils. It is amazing that pupils collude with such a system – even when they work against them. As such we quickly assume an identity as a 'clever', 'naughty', 'stroppy' or 'boring' pupil. Part of this casting is due to early judgements made by teachers and our peers about us and part of it is due to innate self-perception. The situation is made worse if you had the misfortune to grow up in an area with a 'selective' school system and where you might have been told at the age of 11 that you were not bright because you failed a school entrance examination such as the '11-plus'. The problem with these sorts of judgements is not just that they stick but also that they were mainly based on faulty information in the first place, as we

discovered in Chapter 2. Judgements about ability were far too frequently made on the basis of how hard you worked or, even worse, how neat your hand-writing was. Educational thinking has moved on so much in the past thirty or so years that these sorts of judgements are less readily made by teachers now. Judgements by pupils about other pupils are still as strong as ever, though, so that success is often denoted by girls who are pretty and boys who are good at sport. The nice thing for you is that you don't need to worry about any of that now. So ditch your preconceived notions about yourself – they are out of date and unhelpful.

5   The last time that you were in a formal learning situation may have been at school. You may have loved school or you may have loathed it. We will deal with the issue of you as a student in more depth in the next chapter but it is useful at this point to think about how you felt about school because it will have a major influence on how you feel about going back to the classroom as an adult now.

6   As we have already established, although it is tempting to think about learning as just those activities that take place in a school or a college we are mistaken if we do so because we not only continue to learn throughout our lives but also because most of us are learning all the time – in informal as well as formal learning situa-tions. So it may be that you have learned most effectively in recent years by simply sitting next to a competent and sympathetic colleague at work. It is also worth reflecting on how you felt in various working situations. Take some time to con-sider what have been successful learning situations for you at work and where the learning has been less successful. This will help you to continue to build up your profile of your own strengths and weaknesses. In the same way it is also worth reflecting not just on how well you worked with new systems but also on how you dealt with the transitions between jobs and stages in your life. All deep learning involves anxiety because it is about trading an old way of doing things for a new way of doing things. By reflecting on how you have dealt with the anxiety that comes from changing your ways of doing things in the past you will be able to use this knowledge to help you to work in your new learning situation now.

7   So what have you learned over the years? As we have said before, in a world that celebrates youth it is often easy to forget about the sheer pleasure and ease that comes from getting older. It is a cliché, but if you could go back to being 21 you would probably do a lot of things differently. The point is, of course, that we only know what we know now because we have been through what we went through back then. As long as we learn from our experiences then they are a rich source of knowledge about how to deal with the world and to develop protection from it. They allow us to make informed decisions in our thirties, fifties or nineties

because we have had similar experiences before. And if we pause for a minute or so to reflect what we have learned we can begin to see a pattern to the painful experiences and to understand why we had to learn whatever it was we had to learn in a small way in order to protect ourselves in a far bigger way in the future. If we let it, life will provide its own lessons that work like inoculations – giving you just a shot of pain that feels terrible at the time but gives you immunity from a far greater potential pain of the same type later on.

As we discovered in Chapter 3, it is really important to remember the value of wisdom when we talk about the specific skills and knowledge involved in adult learning. Wisdom is precious, and if you allow it to it can help you in all sorts of ways in your new course. Wisdom cannot be bought. Try to think about what you bring to a learning experience – that is part of what you can offer the learning community. No learning happens in a vacuum, and the more rich life experiences you have the more you have to contribute. It is a major advantage that you have over your younger colleagues.

Stage 3

Now we will look at the ways that you might use your answers to the questions above to build your learning plan. Remember that all autobiographies are individual. Your autobiography is unique to your lived experience. It is very difficult, therefore, to classify your answers in this chapter in the same way that we did in previous chapters. You might have had a really good experience at school but you may have had more difficult experiences ever since. You may have written that your mum was always very encouraging and supportive but that you were always very aware of your 'clever' older brother. It is possible to draw some general pointers from the findings, though, and these are given below. First look back at your answers and try to identify whether any patterns emerge or any words or phrases are used repeatedly (such as words relating to ability or lack of it, or words relating to failure or competition).

Advice is given below on three particular themes that may emerge. You may well find that the patterns you have identified fall into more than one of these categories. If this is the case, then simply read all the sections that apply. The most common themes that are unhelpful to learning are:

- **I am not naturally very intelligent.**

- **I am always worried that I might disappoint people.**

- **I am here because of someone's mistake – I am not worthy to be on this course with all of these intelligent people.**

I am not intelligent   Rubbish! Who says that you are not intelligent? So many of the educational assumptions about intelligence have been turned on their heads in the past few decades that it is almost impossible to uphold the judgements that were made about your ability 20 or 30 years ago. As we saw in the earlier chapters, some educationalists have argued convincingly that the old IQ tests only examine a very narrow type of intelligence. The huge advances in brain scanning technology of the past decade have also shown how complex and brilliant an organ the human brain is and that none of us has the authority to make decisions about our own or other people's intelligence, especially as these decisions affect other people for the rest of their lives.

I cannot live up to other people's expectations   If this has been a dominant theme in your life then now is the time to get rid of it. Deciding to learn something is one of the bravest decisions that we make and it is hard enough to make without complicating the issue even more by listening to the voices of others (dead or alive) about what you should be doing. Most parents project expectations onto their offspring and for many these are a mixture of good intentions and their own unfulfilled expectations for life. Again, now is the time to recognize these expectations and if they are not helpful then get rid of them. Your dad may very well have wanted you to go to university at 18 but there was a good reason why you didn't and it's your life. Your chance is now, so take it. Your auntie may well have thought that all women should give up ambitions for a career and devote themselves to their families but she didn't have to struggle to pay for a mortgage and maybe it suited her not to study for anything because she wasn't very academic. Parents, and teachers for that matter, may have been highly influential at the time but now that you have access to different information you will be able to see that some of the assessments that were made about you as a person were probably based on faulty and patchy evidence. Learn to identify where the influences are coming from and ask yourself why it was in these people's interest to place these expectations on you. Then let them go.

I shouldn't be here – I'm an impostor – when they find out how stupid I am then they will throw me off the course   Oh please! There are stringent administrative checks involved in a whole range of courses. If somebody has given you a place on the course then the chances are that they think you are capable of doing the work. This is a completely destructive and ultimately exhausting way of thinking. One way or another you are telling yourself 'I am bad' and then justifying your reasons for thinking this. We will return again to the idea of confidence, but at this stage you need to identify where you have got this idea from and why you still buy into it. Dorothy Rowe (see the suggestions in the Further Reading section below) has written extensively about why children grow up with the idea that they are bad and I recommend that you read her ideas if you are interested in understanding this thought pattern in more depth. In terms of practical ways around it, though, you need to learn to trust the judgements of those who run the courses and who teach you. Put quite simply, if your teachers did not think that you were capable of succeeding they would not have taken you on. It is simply too much hassle to give somebody a place on a course and then have to fail them or counsel them off. It is also very expensive for the institution.

The final word is that we all have various influences on the decisions we make about the way we lead our lives. Some of these emerge from present situations and others are leftovers from our early experiences. There was not much that we could do to change these ideas in the past, but we can now. It's your choice. Let them go.

Further Reading

- You might find it interesting to look at Dorothy Rowe's work. *Beyond Fear* on how to overcome anxieties that have been learned from early experiences but which manifest themselves as attached to present situations. (New York: HarperCollins, 2002) It is a detailed account of how fears are born out of negative ways of constructing your self and your place in the world.

- Burr and Butt (2004) argue that (p. 82) 'We feel threatened when events rock the foundation stones of our construct system. The constructs which are superordinate for us are the ones that define the core of our identity, without which we would have little concept of ourselves as people. They are also the constructs which are fundamental to the way that we make sense of our world, and we may trace back many of our superordinate constructs to this source, like tributaries of a great river.'

- Have a look at Oliver James's (2002) book *They F*** You Up: How to Survive Family Life* (London: Bloomsbury, 2002). In it he develops the argument that parents and carers ascribe rigid roles or 'scripts' to children that can last throughout a lifetime.

7 What Sort of Student Are You?

Aims of the chapter

- In this chapter we will examine how the ideas that formed your identity as a school-aged student (explored in Chapter 6) might have a bearing on the way that you study now and also how you relate to students and tutors
- The main point of this chapter is to illustrate that it is possible to learn how to be a successful student by adopting certain strategies – just like you might learn how to drive a car or learn another language
- In this chapter we will also return to and develop the theme of confidence begun in Chapter 4. It will provide you with some ideas about how to use the useful ideas about learning that you gained at school and also how to get rid of the ones that are less helpful

So far we have discovered what your preferred learning and study style preferences are as well as you bias towards introversion or extraversion. We have also looked at the way that particular life events concerning learning (with a particular focus on your experience of school) have contributed to the way that you construct learning – and what studying means to you. Before we move on to the very specific and practical advice about how to tackle particular areas of study, we will pause to consider how all of this information can lead to a clearer picture of how you operate as a student now – as an adult – and how to get the best out of learning situations.

What's your story?

In previous chapters we established that our experiences of school and study contribute to the way that we regard current learning experiences. Our autobiographies are the stories that we tell ourselves and others about our lives. Stories are very powerful because they shape our understanding of reality. A lot of stories are formed without us really knowing it. By identifying what the story is, we can begin to consider and change the script. It is important to appraise the stories we tell ourselves about our lives as far as learning is concerned because by doing so we can begin to think about why we are making decisions and act to change those ideas.

We all have very strong ideas about ourselves in relation to learning in formal situations that were forged when we were at school. Many of these will be overtly forgotten. But these ideas will contribute to the way that we see the learning because when we are back in similar situations we will revert to the old ways. Although the context will be entirely different, the situation itself may ring bells. Studying for a course may involve sitting in a classroom for the first time in years, for example. In fact, you may feel that you have literally gone back to school. Without realizing it, many of your feelings about being taught and doing homework and getting on with other students may be reawakened.

These relationships are key to your success as a learner and by understanding our student identities we can begin to understand how we draw strength from, as well as limit the damage potentially caused by, such behaviour. All identities have good and bad aspects and by managing our reactions to things we can make as much advantage as we can of studying.

Relationships with tutors and other students

Relationships with tutors and other students also have the power to turn the learning experience into a long, hard slog – even threaten to destroy it altogether when things go wrong – or to make it a fun, life-enhancing experience. Some of this will be down to luck – you cannot choose who teaches you and who you can work with – and some of this is down to your management of the situation.

When things do go wrong your first response may be to try to change the external situation (tutor or group, for example). Literally changing the situation is often not the practical option (although we will look at possible ways that this might be done in the final chapter). Most courses work on a strict student/teacher ratio and this means that a request for a change will often not be met with encouragement. You may also run the risk of antagonizing the tutors. It can be quite difficult to 'come back' from such situations because if you distance yourself from the group and the tutor you may find yourself in an isolated position. It is usually far better to put some thought into changing the relationships rather than the people themselves. The spirit of effective, independent learning suggests that becoming a self-directed, autonomous learner means shifting your focus away from seeing your tutors as your main source of knowledge and beginning to see them as guides – pointing you in the right direction where necessary. You are your main resource and you have access to a world of literature and reference material through libraries, the Internet and the media, if you want it.

Changing the script

By thinking about how our identities are shaped by life experiences we can also begin to understand how these identities can be changed by reappraising them in the light of current circumstances. In this way we can think much more strategically about our learning and begin to alter our behaviour accordingly to encompass new ways of thinking. We do not need to be trapped into ways of working that were established years ago in a completely different context; we can change them.

Look at Cheryl's story. It shows how she was able to get over early disappointments in her education and to draw on her professional successes to help with her adult learning. She had returned to education after many years in industry.

Case Study

Cheryl's story

School

Cheryl was desperately shy at secondary school but she had enjoyed primary school immensely. She had worked extremely hard, and managed to gain an assisted place at a local independent school when she was 11 years old. Her family were very proud of her place at the school, but once she was there things went from bad to worse. She always felt as if she had to run hard just to keep up with the pack. She became more and more withdrawn and increasingly intimidated by the sophisticated and seemingly clever girls who treated her with contempt. Estranged from her old friends on the estate (who had gone to the comprehensive school nearby) but finding no likeminded companionship at her own school she sank further and further into a gloom about school and left at 16 with no qualifications other than a grade C for English Language O Level.

Work

She got her first job quickly after leaving school in the accounts section of a local building firm. There she quickly understood the systems and within a year she had her first promotion. She enjoyed working with all the men. She stayed with the firm, was promoted several times and so by the time she was 30 she was managing the whole operation and was known as the 'brains' of the outfit. At 34 Cheryl left work to have twins, returning at first part-time but she found the hectic juggling of priorities too demanding and so she gave up work altogether. When her children were old enough to attend school she became bored and frustrated at home and she decided to embark on a career change and to find a new job in education.

Return to learning

Cheryl started to study on a learning support assistant training course at her local college. Faced with a room full of women Cheryl found her old identity of the shy, unconfident girl come flooding back. She found it incredibly difficult to 'get in' to any of the groups of friends and the feelings of anxiety meant that she found the lectures very hard to follow. Suddenly it seemed that the 20 years of confident, high achievement in the building industry seemed to slip away from her without a trace – before she knew it she was back in her school classroom. By thinking about her learning autobiography Cheryl was able to recognize the triggers that were pushing her back into her old identity and to look at the situation from more of a distance. She reminded herself that this was an old identity for which she no longer had a purpose and instead she settled into the new process of learning as an adult – free from the problems of the past.

end of case study

What Cheryl's story demonstrates is that you do not need to be a hostage to the patterns of behaviour that were established in the past. With her numerous years of experience in industry behind her, Cheryl had much more to bring to the course than she would have done as a 20-year-old. Try to find ways of using the assets that you have and the things that you have learned from your experience of life to help with your learning as an adult.

Confidence

Self-confidence comes not from perfection – that is always an illusion anyway – but from understanding ourselves as far as possible and by appraising situations in the light of that understanding. We all have limitations and strengths and we plan our activities accordingly. In terms of relationships with teaching staff and fellow students this means developing the ability to learn from others where we can and not taking things personally when they go less well. Our self-confidence tends to dip when we are in situations where we feel distanced or cut off from our objectives and the group with whom we identify; or we lose a sense of control. There are clearly rich possibilities for both in a new adult learning situation.

On the one hand the course and all that goes with it will be a new situation with inherent systems and established ways of doing things that are beyond our control. Learning is an unpredictable activity that always involves change – these are the sort of conditions that are ripe for feelings of anxiety and loss of control.

On the other hand you will be invited to join a group, perhaps for the first time in years, which is not of your own making. Feelings of not fitting in and perhaps not feeling worthy abound. The following ideas should help you to examine those feelings of anxiety that are provoked by these situations by helping you to build up strong and nurturing relationships and helping you to get to a feeling of control – if not complete control – over the learning situation.

What sort of student are you now?

We will start by establishing what sort of student you are, based on past experiences. As with all the other self-assessment exercises in this book, the results are purely indicative and they are designed to help you to see yourself more objectively on the one hand and to help you to make plans and progress on the other. These exercises and results describe behaviour, not innate characteristics. Try to be honest and rapid with your answers, try not to give the answer that you think is correct – instead think of something that really represents the way that you would act.

This self-assessment exercise will help you to overcome problems associated with the way that you deal with tutors, other students and deadlines.

What Sort of Student Are You?

Answer A, B, C, D or E to each question

1 You know that a deadline for an assignment is approaching. Workload and/or family commitments have meant that you have had very little time to spend on the work. What do you do?
A Keep quiet and wait until challenged, then tell the lecturer how busy you have been.
B Not turn up on the handing in day and hope that nobody will notice.
C Decide to forgo the family gathering and stay up until 3.00am finishing the work.
D Tell the lecturer about your situation and offer to hand in all your rough notes with the essay following in a couple of weeks' time.
E None of the above.

2 Your second assignment fails. How do you feel?
A Angry after how hard you have worked; you think seriously about giving up the course.
B Not surprised because you didn't put a great deal of effort into the work. You accept advice on how to improve the work from the lecturer and hope for a better result next time.
C Really depressed and stupid; you knew that this course was above you.

(Continued)

(Continued)

D   Confused; you had thought that you had written a really good essay. Your heart sinks at the long list of boring guidelines that your lecturer has provided you with in order to get it right.

E   None of the above.

3   You can't follow the points in a lecture because it is very intellectual and rambling and it seems unprepared. What do you do?

A   Make conversation with other students quietly at the back of the class. It makes you angry that you have given up so much to do this course and the lecturer can't even be bothered to put any effort in to his teaching.

B   Try to get the lecturer to bring his ideas down to earth by introducing a personal anecdote into the discussion or by asking a practical question.

C   Try hard to concentrate as much as you can. But looking around the room you can see that everybody else is keeping up and this makes you panic. You resolve to stay up late and read all the notes until you understand them.

D   Although the lecture is hard to follow and some of the points are a bit obscure they set you off thinking about a related and more interesting topic. Your thoughts absorb you for the rest of the lecture.

E   None of the above.

4   Think back to when you were at secondary school. Think of the teacher who you got on best with. Back then, which of the following statements would he have made about you?

A   That you were a natural leader who spoke up well when things concerned you.

B   That you were a really popular member of the group who always contributed to discussions and added to a happy, fun environment in lessons.

C   That you were a pleasure to teach and that you worked very hard.

D   That you had talent and a sparkiness that set you out from the rest of the group.

E   None of the above.

5   Now think of the teacher with whom you had the most disputes. What would he have said?

A   That you were stroppy and uncooperative.

B   That you were unreliable and did not do your homework.

C   That you were unresponsive in class (he might not even know who you were).

D   That you were a bit arrogant – deliberately not fitting in with the system, or that you were more interested in what was going on in your head than what was happening in the classroom.

E   None of the above.

(Continued)

(Continued)

6   Think of the subject that you least enjoyed at school. Which of the following statements best describes your behaviour in lessons?

A   Conflict with the teacher – you were often sent out or walked out of lessons.

B   You didn't turn up if you could manage it and if you did you managed not to be really involved in the lesson (you would be reading a magazine, for example).

C   You were withdrawn and unhappy in lessons and until this day you still feel useless at that subject – you gave it up as soon as you possibly could.

D   You felt contempt for the subject and for those who taught it. You spent the time doing something else.

E   None of the above.

7   What was your attitude to exams?

A   You had very little confidence about your ability to pass them so you tended not to revise. You resented doing them and you hated sitting in silence for two hours on end.

B   You felt really upset by them. They always seemed to crop up without warning and you'd be really anxious – it was pot luck whether you passed or not.

C   You revised really hard and you did well in most of them. You might be sick with anxiety on the night before.

D   You did brilliantly in the things that interested you – you often felt that you could write for ever on those topics. You actually enjoyed the challenge of writing for such a concentrated period of time – it was good not to have the distractions. In other subjects where you had little interest you put no effort into revising at all and didn't mind failing.

E   None of the above.

8   What is your biggest fear regarding your present study?

A   Being thrown off the course because I'm not up to it (intellectually or personally).

B   Failing all the essays because I can't find the time.

C   Being found out that I can only do what I can because I work hard. If I stop working so hard everyone will know that I'm thick.

D   Finding out that I have chosen the wrong course and that it has all been a waste of time.

E   None of the above.

9   Regarding your present study, you notice that your lecturer never makes eye contact with you and she is never as friendly to you as she is to other people. How do you react?

(Continued)

(Continued)

A   Take it personally and be just as unfriendly back.

B   Be extra charming in breaks and ask questions to make sure she notices you.

C   Feel sorry for her – it must be so difficult to catch everybody's eye in such a big group.

D   It confirms your feeling that you have nothing in common with the tutor or the subject so you give up listening and get on with planning your essay rather than taking notes.

E   None of the above.

10   In terms of studying (rather than socializing) at school, when were you happiest?

A   In situations where you were allowed to use your maturity and to draw on the skills that you had developed outside school. Perhaps this was on outside trips, organizing enterprise activities and work experience – things that you particularly enjoyed because you weren't treated like a child at those points.

B   In lively discussions in lessons.

C   In traditional lessons with kind teachers who had strict boundaries about deadlines and high standards, where there was order.

D   When you could go off at a tangent – drawing ideas from a range of sources and linking your hobbies and interests from outside school to what you did inside.

E   None of the above.

11   What was your attitude to homework?

A   You put a lot of effort in at first. If it paid off then that was great, if not you wouldn't bother to try hard again.

B   You rarely did it.

C   You worked really hard at it – even if you didn't like the subject.

D   You could spend hours on something that interested you but you couldn't be bothered with things that bored you.

E   None of the above.

12   In terms of things that teachers/lecturers do, which of the following annoy you the most?

A   Someone who patronizes you and makes you feel small.

B   Someone who doesn't learn names or make any effort to include people in discussions.

C   Someone who sets a deadline and then lets others off or forgets it.

(Continued)

(Continued)

D Someone who is rigidly small-minded.

E None of the above.

Count your answers in As, Bs, Cs, Ds and Es

Analysis of Your Results

Your answers to the questions will have put you into one of these caregories:

Mostly A = Combatant

Mostly B = Avoidant

Mostly C = Compliant

Mostly D = Maverick

Mostly E = Unidentified type – it may mean that you have already developed a good range of strategies that are available to you or it may mean that you are having some difficulty in engaging with the idea of thinking about learning.

Mostly A – the combatant

You are a strong, independently minded person and your energy and sense of justice are truly impressive. At your best you can contribute masses of insight to a topic and you have a very special asset – an ability to think for yourself. When you are feeling less secure, though, you can be a little too readily drawn to conflict in a way that gets you into trouble. Your challenge is to become more reflective. You have a lot to offer and the learning will allow you to achieve much more by helping you to hone those skills of analysis to a finer level. Try to spot the situations where you may feel vulnerable – working with a tutor who seems to be ignoring or undermining you, for example, and take preventative action to ensure that the situation does not escalate into a conflict. The first thing to do in these situations is to cease being so defensive. Be honest with yourself about where your weaknesses lie and bite your tongue and think for a while each time you feel compelled to complain about something. You tend to take things personally – taking offence easily. You need firm boundaries and guidelines and part of your challenge is to learn to impose them on yourself rather than forcing others into authority figure positions. Your strengths are that you work well with kindly and encouraging tutors who help you to harness those strong reactions and your enormous capacity for energy and independent thought.

Some of the most effective people in the world fall into this category: think about those people who have changed the way that we look at poverty in the economically developing world or women's rights, for example, and you will see the enormous amount that can be achieved by someone of this ilk.

(Continued)

(Continued)

Strengths	Weaknesses
You can get on well with other students – you have a well-founded sense of what is right and wrong and you will stand up for others who are being treated unfairly	You lack the real confidence that makes you impervious to unhelpful criticism
	You can have difficulty in reflecting on yourself
You are tough and resilient	You are quick to blame others
You have a lot of personal experience to draw on	You move to hostility quickly
	You find it difficult to admit fault – and so move on
You have tremendous courage	
You are easily able to engage in critical thought	

Mostly B – the avoidant

You are able to contribute enormously to experiential and socially constructed learning situations because your well-developed social skills make you a popular colleague and student. When things go well you are enormously creative and your enjoyment of the learning can be very beneficial to the group. You make valuable contributions to discussions and your gift for communication and sense of fun can help to create a lovely, relaxed atmosphere in situations that might otherwise be confrontational. When you are feeling more vulnerable, though, you tend to find ways of avoiding the challenging situation.

If you are an avoidant ask yourself why you decided to take up study on the programme in the first place. Try to think about your studies in more adult terms. Your tendency is to behave rather like a teenager might in a situation when he or she is being asked to do something that is unappealing – you tend to remove yourself from whatever it is that is hassling you. Adult education lecturers do not have the same expectations of behaviour management and discipline as school teachers do. Your attempts to place your lecturer in a position of disciplinarian are likely to be met with bemusement or irritation. Go back to the chapter on motivation and work out a reward system to help you move on.

Strengths	Weaknesses
You have generally good relationships with the other students	You find it very difficult to meet deadlines

(Continued)

(Continued)

You often have good relationships with some tutors whose teaching style suits the way that you work

You enjoy the discussion-based sessions and you have a lot to contribute

Verbally you are very strong

You make connections between theory and practice easily

You may feel hemmed in by too much structure

You can exhibit a tendency to 'cast' tutors as punitive authority figures and jeopardize your relationships with them

You often get your priorities mixed up

You find it quite easy to make excuses. All of these aspects can lead to hostility and confrontation – neither of which you enjoy

Mostly Cs – the compliant

Be kind to yourself! You have enormous potential to be excellent but only if you can slow down for long enough to enjoy the ride. Yours is the opposite behaviour to category A – you always blame yourself first and then others. Your challenge is to accept being just good enough rather than aiming for perfection all the time. Try to allow yourself some less than perfect moments in the short term in order to get long-term payoff and stamina. Also try to rationalize more difficult situations by thinking less in terms of blame and more in terms of cause and effect. If you score a low grade for an assignment then an understanding that it coincided with a par-ticularly demanding time at work and your mother's bout of serious illness should help you to see why you achieved a lower grade than usual, to see this 'under-achievement' in terms of the bigger picture of your work on the course.

Many people in this category were brought up in very authoritarian households. This meant that rules were taken very seriously indeed and there was no room at all for non-compliance and rebellion. If this is the case then you may often find yourself aghast at the way that other people challenge systems and people in positions of authority in the system. This may have served you well because it meant that you rarely got into trouble or made enemies of bosses or teachers. This tendency will hinder your learning now, though, if you do not challenge the assumptions that underpin your thoughts because critical thought is essential to higher-level study. Also, try to understand that people in authority positions – including tutors – are only human and so often make mistakes. If you point this out to them it will not result in the end of the world as we know it! You are a lovely person with the tact and social skills that many others lack. You will continue to be a lovely person if you develop the confidence to challenge – so go ahead and be kind to yourself and more ques-tioning of others.

(Continued)

(Continued)

Strengths	Weaknesses
You meet all deadlines	You tend to blame yourself when things go wrong
Your attendance and punctuality records are excellent	You are sometimes in danger of losing sight of the bigger picture in your pursuit of details
You do everything that is asked of you	You can work so hard on particular tasks that your overall performance suffers
Your written work is good	You can be over-earnest in sessions and so miss the fun and support of the group
You work very hard	Your biggest danger is burn out
You are a self-starter – even in trying circumstances	You set yourself such high standards that you can easily get disillusioned when things go less well

Mostly Ds – the maverick

You are a truly independent thinker and you gain a good deal of pleasure and a sense of achievement from working on your own. More than any other type, you are able to motivate yourself and to use your own sense of standards to measure your own progress.

If you are a maverick then your main challenge is to hold on to your originality while operating within a constraining system. When harnessed properly your gift for original thought can be a real boon. Your challenge is first to make sure that you understand exactly what is being asked of you and then to make the effort to work with other students. You understand the bigger picture rather better than any of the other types of students but this means that you sometimes tend to neglect the details. It would be fair to say that you even despise detail and whilst this is fine when you are grappling with concepts, it will bring your grades down to a lower level than you deserve in your written work – so force yourself to look at the details as well.

Strengths	Weaknesses
You are a supreme self-starter – you have lots of initiative	You are often rather distanced from the other students and this means that you can miss out on the enormous resource that the group can provide
You are able to take information from a range of sources and synthesize it	You feel very constrained by systems and prescriptive formats for work – you can reject them out of hand to your own cost

(Continued)

(Continued)

Your capacity for originality gives you the potential to be brilliant	You can be a bit off the wall – sometimes missing the point
You are less put off by external limitations (less than perfect teaching, for example) than the other types because you work so well under your own steam	You can let bureaucracy get on top of you – demonizing it – and you sometimes miss out on the potential it has to help with organization
You provide new and fresh perspectives that help everyone to see things differently	You can dismiss things out of hand that do not interest you

Mostly Es – unidentified type

All of the other types outlined above are stances that we can adopt at appropriate moments. They do not describe genetic dispositions but rather ways of working which we may have adopted through repetition and which now have become a habit. If you answered 'none of the above' to most of the questions there are two possible interpretations. It may be because you are already a mature, independent learner. If so, congratulations – you are diplomatic and reflective and whether these are skills that you have always had or ones that you have developed in recent years they will serve you well as an adult learner. You are also able to strike a good balance between self-reflection and the ability to make positive criticisms of the course and its material. You have learned a good deal from your previous experiences and they have served you well. The second interpretation is that you feel so distanced from the learning situations in which you find yourself that it is very difficult for you to categorize your behaviour in this way. You are not experiencing sufficient coherence in your learning to perceive patterns yet. If this is the case, then your aim is to try to develop a more reflective approach to learning. Try to slow down so that you can begin to observe the decisions you make about how to act rather than being so caught up in those actions that you cannot see that there are alternative paths to follow. Remember that resilient and effective learners draw from a repertoire of responses in different situations and tell yourself that there is always more than one way of interpreting a situation and reacting to it.

Whatever category you fall into, it is worth remembering that a life lived is the most precious resource at our disposal – if only we can reflect on it. A lot of the ways that we behave are the result of subconscious impulses born from previous experience. The main thing to remember now is that you can avert those thoughts and impulses and change the repetitive patterns that have become habits. By combining the knowledge of your student type with your understanding of your learning style, study style and intuitive style you can equip yourself to encounter the most challenging of learning experiences.

The student – tutor relationship

Although there are similarities between the relationships we have with our teachers at school and the relationships we have with college tutors, there is a good deal that is different. There is still a level of expectation and conformity that you would expect but it is much looser as an adult. At the end of the day, as an adult, if you do not work hard, nobody is going to chase you for the work – you will simply fail the course. It is a harsh fact but you will need to remember it at all times. Tutors are also adults and human beings and they will resist your attempts to put them into authority positions. The best way to deal with them is not to antagonize them but to put yourself in their position. Use your understanding of your student type to guide the way that you act in relationship with your tutors. As you will know, although most of the people that you encounter will be personable and well-meaning, a minority of tutors will be difficult to get on with, despite all your best efforts. My advice in this situation is that you keep your head down and get on with the course as much as possible unless there is something truly amiss. If you really feel that you have been humiliated by a tutor it is always best to approach him or her to explain how your feelings have been hurt, rather than involving any third parties. Most tutors will respond to this well and provide you with some explanation. At least your own self-respect will be restored – even if the teaching does not improve as a result.

The student–student relationship

Nobody would suggest that you need to like everyone in the group. Part of the learning process is working with others. Try to apply the ideas that we have covered in the rest of the book about your own learning to others. The points about levels of confidence, learning styles and strengths and weaknesses are equally true for the other students as they are for you. Do not automatically assume that just because one of the other students in your group talks a lot, that she is very confident; some people deal with their own anxieties by talking a lot – others simply have very good verbal skills. The important thing to remember is that any course of learning will involve a repertoire of various skills and abilities and that people shine in different situations. Just because you are more nervous in a class situation, it does not mean that you will not score very highly in the written work. Get to know your own strengths and weaknesses to anticipate where aspects of the learning that might be difficult for you might lie and plan accordingly. Having said that, it is very important that you do make an effort to take part in the group discussions if you are shy. Not only does talking provide a social function (it binds the group together and it means that everybody can develop a 'voice' within the group), but also talking is an essential to the learning process. Only by articulating our understanding and meaning can we help it to progress. If you repeatedly opt out of group discussion activities you will be depriving yourself of this very rich form of learning.

The repertoire of strategies

All of the categories we looked at (A–D) have their strengths in the right situation. Confidence comes from knowing how to read situations and from having a range of strategies to deal with the learning. It also means moving to a position where we make conscious choices and we are optimistic about the outcomes of those choices. As confident, reflective learners we are happy to take responsibility for the choice and the action but also understand that we may lose control of the outcomes once the action has been carried out in good faith.

In this chapter we have established that there are a range of behaviours available to you as a student. We have also discussed the ways that you can build your own confidence by accessing a range of your strengths and weaknesses. In the next chapter we will look at ways that you can put these ideas into practical use in terms of writing essays, taking part in tutorials and doing presentations to the group.

Further Reading

- One of the key thinkers about adult education was Edward Lindeman. He argued that the strength of the adult learner is his or her own experience of the world and that we should look into the 'reservoirs' of our experience to apply what needs to be learned before looking at the subject in hand. If you are interested in reading more about the origins of thinking about modern adult education you could look at Lindeman, E.H. (1928) *The Meaning of Adult Education* (New York: New Republic).

- Malcolm Knowles also stresses the centrality of the student experience. His use of the word andragogy to describe adult learning separates it from pedagogy which is used to describe learning by children. He also argues that the experience of adult learning has significant differences from childhood education and in particular this is linked to the use of previous life experience in the learning situation. See Knowles, M.S., *The Modern Practice of Adult Education: From Andragogy to Pedagogy* (Chicago: Follett Publishing, 1980).

- Daniel Goleman's work on emotional intelligence stresses the benefits of learning to recognize and name our emotions in response to situations. Have a look at *Working with Emotional Intelligence* (London: Bloomsbury, 1998). Although this work deals with the workplace, there is a good deal in it that is relevant to adult learners in general.

8 Putting Effective Learning into Practice

This chapter will:

- Explain how to make sense of assessment grids and how to use them to enhance your performance
- Give practical advice about how to tackle the various forms of writing that you may be asked to complete – including academic tasks such as the traditional assignment and the professional task such as the portfolio
- Offer advice for giving presentations
- Provide help for the business of meeting deadlines and achieving the required tasks
- Help you to think about retrieving a situation that has gone wrong

By now you should have a good understanding of where your particular strengths lie and also where you could develop your skills. The sorts of tasks that will be required of you in any course of study will usually involve a great deal of reading, a fair amount of writing and differing proportions of listening to lectures, observing professional practice (depending on the course) and finding things out for yourself in the library or on the Internet. By using your knowledge about your own personal study style you can ensure that you get the best out of all these activities.

Measuring your own learning and responding to grades and assessments

When working on an accredited course we tend to mark and measure our progress according to the grades we are awarded for each of the modules or stages of the course. Sometimes we can perceive a natural improvement or pattern in the grades – they may improve as you get further into the course – and sometimes there seems to be no pattern at all because the grades seem to be all over the place. Ideally you need to be able to shift your perception away from the grades as decided by other people and move towards an understanding of your own academic progress that is underpinned by a deep and genuine appreciation of what is needed to improve your work and this is informed by, but not limited by, your tutors' grades. We often mistakenly see the graded outcome of a module – the assessment – as completely separate from the learning process itself. It is much more useful to develop an understanding of an assessment as something that has an ongoing, organic relationship with the learning. You can do this by spending time getting to understand the assessment criteria (ask to have a copy if it is not provided) and making the effort to apply the criteria to each piece of work that you do before you submit it. So if your assessment criteria suggest that you need to respond critically to research texts in order to gain a grade B or above, you need to take the responsibility to ask your tutors what this means and really make sure that you have grasped the concept. Once you have done that you need to critically appraise any written work that you have done and ask yourself in a detached, dispassionate way, whether or not you have met these criteria. In other words, don't just leave it to chance!

Here is a quick guide to de-mystifying the language of assessment grids:

Clarity	This refers to your level of expression – are the words that you choose and the way that you arrange your sentences helpful to the reader? Are your arguments and points easy to follow? Try reading your whole assignment aloud to make sure that it flows and correct as you go along if it doesn't.
Methods and methodology	If you are conducting a piece of research in the workplace or on a wider scale you will be expected to show that you have thought about the investigative methods that you have chosen to use and give your reasons for choosing them. This means not immediately issuing questionnaires because they seem like the easiest thing to do but instead considering what the benefits of using the questionnaire are in relation to the particular thing that you are looking at (why not use interviews or observation, for example) and defending your decision.
Level of expression	Are your choices of words and phrases appropriate to the level at which you are writing? Try using a thesaurus to extend the range of your vocabulary but don't go overboard and make your sentences more complex than they need to be. Try to avoid colloquialisms and slang (words and phrases such as 'I feel fed up') – they are inappropriate in an academic assignment.
Critical engagement	This means demonstrating that you have really thought about the literature and ideas and considered them in the light of your own experience. Don't be afraid to say when you disagree with something in a text and make it clear when you agree with a theoretical point of view.
Analysis	Analysis literally means taking something apart – this means getting to what is behind a question and understanding the assumptions in a point of view.

Ethical code   If you are carrying out a research project or writing a report in your place of work you will need to ensure that everybody who participates knows exactly what they are agreeing to be involved in and you should guarantee anonymity – this means no names of institutions or individuals.

Reflection   Show that you have thought about the issues that you are dealing with in the assignment and that you are not just accepting the views that you have been presented with. Also try to show that you are developing your ideas as you go along and that you are willing to be tentative and try out ideas and think about the results.

Links between theory and practice   Make it clear that you are thinking about what you have read in the light of what you are experiencing in the workplace and vice versa. Try to avoid dividing your writing into clear sections in which you deal with theory in the first part and the realities of practice in the second. Instead try to let the theory structure your thinking throughout the writing.

Literature review   This is where you demonstrate that you have spent the time in the library and that you fully understand the issues that you are writing about. Try to use a literature review section to show that you have reflected on a wide variety of points of view and remember to reflect on the ideas all the way through your writing.

Logical argument   Make sure that all your ideas follow on from each other in a way that makes sense. A clear argument should flow throughout your writing.

Conclusions   This is both the final section of the assignment and the way that you present your findings from the study. Use this section to show what you have learned from doing the project as well as considering the ideas presented in the writing itself.

Presentation   This has a wider meaning than just what the assignment looks like. Although the way that the typing looks on the page is important – make sure that you have followed all the guidelines regarding font size and spacing – you also need to ensure that all the referencing and the bibliography correspond to the guidelines that you have been given.

Completing academic tasks

With academic tasks the criteria and level of expectation are particularly important. Many courses will merge the academic and professional tasks but for the purposes of simplicity they have been divided into academic tasks (involving all forms of extended writing and formal discussion) and professional tasks (involving all forms of presentation, report writing and the gathering of evidence for portfolios).

Writing assignments and dissertations

Among the most daunting of tasks for any adult student is the prospect of writing at length – a traditional essay or an assignment or a report. Even (perhaps especially) the most highly achieving students go through a period of uncertainty and doubt in the weeks between having the assignment set and actually beginning it. The reasons for this are many. It is partly connected to the length of time since the student wrote in a formal, academic way; in general, the longer the gap the greater the anxiety. It is also partly connected to the way that we understand writing to be a revelation of our true selves and, ultimately, our worth. This is partly true, because writing does come from within ourselves and only we can be completely responsible for it, but it is not the whole story. Writing is also just a skill in the same way that working out arithmetic or drawing a map are skills, and there are plenty of different ways and modes of writing. One of the benefits of working on a course is that you can begin to understand how to pick from a repertoire of learning styles that you have available to you and to move away from the position where there is only one way of writing.

Guidelines for writing assignments   There are plenty of very good books on the process of writing itself (see the Further Reading section at the end of the chapter) and ways that you can improve your writing. In my experience as a tutor, though, once most people have got started with the writing they are able to work quite well on their own and even where they have problems they can usually work with the tutor's advice for corrective action. Rather, it is overcoming the psychological barriers at the beginning of the work that is the most problematic for most people. The following ideas are to help you with that awful stage of staring at a blank piece of paper and wondering how on earth you are going to fill it with 3,000 words or so.

Try to bear the following points in mind when you are trying to get started with an extended piece of writing.

- The link between writing and thought is strong. Writing is not just the outcome of thoughts that you have already had; the act of writing helps you to think about things in new ways and to take your thoughts to a much deeper level. Try seeing the writing as the main learning activity rather than a demonstration of learning that has already taken place – this will help you to see value in the activity.

- Think of writing like cooking – the longer that you can give to the process the richer and more rewarding the result. For this reason get going with an assignment as soon after it is set as possible – by making notes and assembling a plan at an early stage you will get your brain thinking at a deeper level that you can return to and explore as the time goes by.

- A golden rule is to start writing as soon as possible. As we all know from seaside holidays, the longer that you stand on the shore, the colder the water gets, so jump right in as soon as you can. At this stage everything you write can (and probably will) be changed later on so you are not committing yourself to anything.

- Develop a repertoire of writing styles to help with this jumping in. Writing can take the form of planning, note taking and mulling over ideas in fragments. All serve different purposes and all help you to get over the barriers that you may have about writing.

- Give yourself a target in the early stages. When you are experiencing real anxiety about getting started give yourself the target of writing no more than 300 words on the topic. Three hundred words about how *little* you know about the subject and what is so difficult about the question can work wonders for getting you started.

- After the first piece of writing (which may be no more than a statement of anxiety) do nothing to the work for about 24 hours. Leave it and do something unrelated – something that perhaps you will not have time to do once you really get started on the work.

- The following day go back to your piece of writing and this time write the question or title in the middle of a piece of paper and circle it. Now annotate it as fully as you can. Circle the words you don't understand and look them up in reference books, underline the bits that do make sense and add in your initial thoughts about how to deal with them. Write down anything that occurs to you at this stage – no matter how tangential – you can edit out the red herrings afterwards. The point is to get your brain thinking laterally. So the immediate responses to a question such as this one

What do you understand by the term 'accountability' in your own working context?

might include a dictionary definition of the word accountability, a more specific definition from your own working context (perhaps something that you have gained from your course) as well as what the word means to you – have you heard it used by politicians and if so in which contexts? You might also add in things that the word reminds you of, personally. Does it make you think about the word 'accountancy' or 'counting'? If so what do those words mean and are they relevant? Then turn to the words 'working context' and add in what you can think of about your situation – use your imagination at this stage to think really widely. Remember that nobody will see this piece of writing other than you. This is the time to take risks and think creatively. Put all the ideas down – there are no wrong or right answers at this stage.

- Now think about posing a set of smaller (sub) questions that will help you to answer the overall question. Once you have this initial group of ideas try to construct them into a plan. The act of putting them into a plan will help you to filter the good ideas and edit out the duff ones.

- You could use the headings from the plan as a writing frame – so plot them onto pieces of paper (or on the screen if you are working on the computer) and leave gaps for where you are going to write about each topic.

- You are now ready to write, so get going with the first draft.

Taking part in seminars and discussions

Discussing issues in an academic context is one of the most challenging things that you can be asked to do as an adult learner. It is one of those things that, once you have fully mastered it, it is very easy to forget how difficult you once found it, but in the early stages group discussions are incredibly daunting. This is because talking is used to enhance understanding but the talking is also being used in a way that is unfamiliar to other contexts. Ambiguities and uncertainties are not only expected but encouraged. It seems that you are being asked to take contradictory positions at the same time – at once be both tentative but confident while also proving that you are a good listener while also asserting your own point of view. Once you can do it you will find group discussions one of the most enjoyable and enlightening learning experiences available and many people find that this sort of talking and listening comes very naturally to them. If you are not quite there yet, though, here are some guidelines to help you to survive those early nail-biting sessions.

Guidelines for the group discussion novice

- Take the focus away from yourself and try to focus on what the group as a whole is doing and where the discussion is going. *Nobody* else will have you as the main focus – they will either be engaging in the topic or thinking about themselves (or a topic related to themselves but unrelated to the discussion in hand).

- It is a good idea to have a pen and paper to hand so that you can make a note of the ideas as they develop and to write down thoughts as they occur to you. This will help you to keep track of the conversation and add clarity to what you say when you feel confident enough to speak up.

- You can control a group discussion in three ways. You can dominate the talk so all the attention is focused on you, you can introduce new subject matter and so take the discussion in a new direction, or you can slow the discussion down. Clearly the second two are the most valuable in learning situations (don't try the first – you will irritate everybody, not least the tutor). The idea is never to take control permanently but just to assert yourself enough to take control of parts of the discussion.

- Do not be afraid to ask for further explanation if you have not understood a point or if you think that the group is treating a topic in a rather superficial way. Ways to do this are to say, 'Do you mind if we stay with the point that Emma just made for a bit longer – I think there are interesting issues involved' or 'Can we just go back to Alan's idea? The conversation moved on a bit too quickly for me to grasp it – can you say that bit again please, Alan?' You will be amazed by how expressing what seems to you to be uncertainty can give you enormous authority in a group discussion. This is an example of slowing down the discussion – as mentioned above.

- Bide your time before speaking but try not to opt out altogether. Somebody who contributes nothing is nearly as conspicuous as somebody who dominates and you will make your colleagues feel unnerved (because they may feel that you are making judgements about them) and your tutor concerned that you are disengaged or not keeping up.

- All the obvious points about not interrupting and not shouting down or ridiculing other points of view are applicable, but as a nice person you will know that anyway!

- Try to draw from the discussion the points that refer to the bigger picture. It is fine to give a pithy illustration from real life about a point you make but please don't give lengthy anecdotes about your own experiences. It bores everybody and it detracts from the issues in hand. When other people do this (and they will!) try to gently guide them to a more theoretical analysis of what their anecdote has to offer the issue being discussed (your tutor will be delighted with your support).

- Points made about the implications for the wood are much more impressive than those which only refer to the practicalities for the trees: 'I would like to explore how the move to equal opportunities will change and shape the workplace in the next few years' will always be more impressive than 'What if we've got nowhere to put a disabled toilet where I work?'

Completing professional tasks

On some courses some of the tasks that will be set will be professional rather than academic in their nature. These tasks include observations of experienced professionals at their work, experienced professionals observing you, assessment of work and bureaucratic tasks. Many of these tasks will adhere to a different type of assessment criteria and it is a good idea to check right at the beginning what the criteria are. It is also a good idea to take the deadlines and requirements for presentation particularly seriously – you will be judged on this adherence to professional standards just as much as the content itself.

Compiling portfolios

Many courses have the completion of a portfolio as a main requirement for writing. A portfolio will generally include a good deal of evidence about the progress of your professional and theoretical understanding in the workplace. Usually you will be given a set of guidelines to follow about what to include but many of the judgements of which particular pieces of paper to put in and what to leave out will be up to you. This involves a good deal of judicious choice and an ongoing responsibility on your part about keeping data and a record of your work. The onus is on you to take seriously all of your activities so that you have a good choice about what to put in. In general the portfolio will include a range of evidence about your work and development and this will be tied together by a reflective piece of writing in which you explicitly consider your learning and development in the light of particular theoretical perspectives.

The mistake that people tend to make when compiling a portfolio is that they tend to put far too much emphasis on the evidence and far too little emphasis on the reflective account of that evidence. The only point in submitting any of these things as evidence is that your reflections on them indicate learning on your part. To this end it is a good idea to annotate them and to show that you have learned from them. In the same way, how you structure the portfolio is very important.

The range of things that are sometimes included in a portfolio is wide, but commonly they include:

- **Records of observations in the workplace**

- **Assessments of the student's work (by other professionals)**

- **Memos that are pertinent to the subject of the portfolio**

- **Notes and comments on policy documents relating to the work**

- **Notes of meetings and relevant professional conversations**

- **Your comments on a wide range of readings.**

Giving presentations to the group

Preparing a presentation

In terms of the fear that is induced in adult learners, the presentation given to the group is second only to doing an extended piece of writing. In order to give a presentation you will need to make notes and talk from them. Technology has an important and useful role to play in making presentations but it can also make the whole exercise even more daunting than it needs to be, so get to know how confident you feel with the use of technology and make your choice about whether or not to use it accordingly. *Never* use technology to support an important presentation unless you have practised with it beforehand. If you do not have time to practice with an audience, you could use an overhead projector or points already written on a flip chart to demonstrate your ideas. On the other hand, the danger for people who are technologically able is that the technology can obscure the intended meaning of the presentation. If this is the case for you try to aim for explaining your ideas as clearly as possible and avoid indulging in technical wizardry for the sake of it. Try to avoid getting into the trap of reading the work you have done; this can be rather dull for your audience. Try to reduce the main points to either prompts on file cards or on PowerPoint.

Giving a presentation

At the point at which you give the presentation you may well be feeling very nervous. Depending on your previous professional experience this will be a less or more daunting experience. One of the best general rules about giving a presentation is not to read too much into the expressions on people's faces. Most people always have a blank expression – whomever they are listening to – when they are not laughing or smiling but are simply listening. Do not take it personally as a judgement of how boring you are nor how hostile their feelings are towards you. Try to make eye contact with everybody in the room and avoid staring at the clock at the back of the room or at the floor. If you are confident enough to put in a joke at the beginning do so; it helps to put your audience at their ease. But don't go overboard as that can give the impression that you are taking a flippant approach to the presentation and undermine the work that you have put into the preparation.

Writing reports

The style of writing that you use for a written report or a bureaucratic task is more succinct and lucid than that you would use for a theoretical and academic assignment.

A report is an explanation of something that is already happening, usually in the workplace. You are expected to give as clear as possible an account for the reader of a situation that exists. The key is to view the events in a way that makes them understandable to the observer and to write about them in as lucid a way as possible. The planning stages are similar to those for an assignment but you will not have nearly so free a rein to use your imagination. You can bring in all relevant information but you are not expected to think laterally in the same way as you would with an assignment.

Once you have identified what you need to do and have made a plan of all the data that you need to gather from the workplace you can start to write. Remember that just because you are writing about something that is really happening, rather than something that is a set of more abstract ideas (as with an assignment), it does not mean that you can neglect theory – you will be expected to locate all of your ideas and observations in a theoretical context by referring to research that has been completed in similar areas. Whereas most assignments are written in one continuous piece of writing, the report is more likely to be broken up into headed sections and these will normally be numbered into main and sub-sections – such as 1, 1.1, 1.2, 1.3 and 1.4, followed by 2, 2.1 and so on.

Meeting deadlines

Juggling work and home life with a course of study is incredibly demanding and one of the most obvious ways that this manifests itself is in your ability or otherwise to meet deadlines. Part-time study is particularly difficult because you need constantly to make compromises and judgements about what or whom to put first. One of the things you can do that is very useful is to buy and use a diary, putting all your commitments in it – study deadlines, work deadlines and family and friend commitments. You might create a timetable for each of your deadlines so that instead of leaving all of the work until the last minute it is equally spread throughout the time available. Remember that learning is a bit like slow cooking – it takes time for the ideas to sink in and for you to mull over your understanding. For this reason it is always a good idea to take as much of the available time as possible – integrating gaps for you to really get to know what you think about a topic – before handing in the work.

So, a 4,000 word piece of writing about a case study that you observe in your workplace may have a three month lead-in time. Let's say it is set in early January to be handed in at the end of March, giving you 12 weeks to complete it. Let's take as our title

> Investigate the relationship between the customer and the provider in your workplace. Take one particular case study or issue from the past two years to explore in detail how the situation emerged and was resolved.

A week-by-week plan for the workload may look like the one below. You will notice that in addition to the column for the task (literally what you will have to do each week) there is a section for the outcome – that is, what will prove that you have achieved your target. This need not be an outward manifestation (such as the number of words written) – it may just be a deeper level of understanding. It is a good idea to work backwards. So write your accumulated outcome in stages – this is where you want to be at each point over the 12 weeks.

Date (week commencing)	Task	Outcome
January Week 1	Review question and set initial boundaries for the literature review	Make sense of what I am being asked to do
January Week 2	Seek approval from gatekeepers at work and explore area for focus	Set up research at work
January Week 3	Do initial literature review (shallow but find out what is available) Write plan for assignment	Gain wide understanding of the literature available and plan assignment
January Week 4	Begin to gather data from workplace and do reading	Research under way Initial reading done
February Week 5	Rewrite plan – very detailed plan emerges	Full plan – the working plan for the assignment has now emerged

February Week 6	Continue to read and make notes from literature review	Deeper understanding of theoretical issues
February Week 7	Finer reading search and begin to write	Specific information relevant to my study identified
February Week 8	Write	First 1,500 words written
March Week 9	Write	Next 1,500 words (minimum) written
March Week 10	Edit and add in more data and literature if necessary	Text now in region of 4,000 words
March Week 11	Rewrite to take it to a higher level = consult the assessment criteria	Text written at appropriate level
March Week 12	Proofread and complete final draft	All expression and clarity issues have been checked

Dealing with distractions

Many of the distractions that you will come across are ongoing and there is nothing that you can really do about them other than schedule blank time to accommodate them or rearrange your schedule so that they are absorbed into your life by other supporting structures or people. Some distractions are far more serious, though, and many highly successful students have encountered enormous difficulties – bereavement, serious illness and unemployment, for example – and these circumstances have naturally had an enormous effect on the progression of their studies. At these times the wise thing to do is to take a break in your studies – with negotiation with your tutors. You may want to add a final column to the work plan table above in which you forecast distractions (going away for the weekend, your appraisal at work or your child's birthday) so that you can anticipate them and compensate in advance.

What to do when it all goes wrong

Even given the best will in the world and all the most carefully set out plans, there will be times when your schedule falls apart. Here is a guide to the ways that you might take remedial action.

How it goes wrong	*What to do*
Four weeks in advance it looks like you might miss the deadline because of work pressures	This is not so bad. The main thing to do is to contact your tutor, formally, as soon as you are aware that there may be a problem. A letter or an e-mail in which you set out your problem and alert them to the situation and perhaps ask for a meeting to discuss your options, would be a good starting point. Make it clear in the letter or e-mail that you are taking the situation very seriously and that you will do all in your power to meet the deadline. Do not let time pass before acting, even if you think that you may still be able to submit the work.
You miss the deadline because the final weekend that you put aside to work on the assignment is taken up by a minor catastrophe at home	Contact the tutor and explain the situation. Be completely honest and do not embellish the situation in an attempt to add weight to your argument – it will simply look as if you are making excuses. At the same time put into the post a copy of all the coherent work that you have done so far – the first draft and the plan, for example. Attach an accompanying letter in which you re-iterate the apology and confirm that you will send the final version within the week.
You get an assignment back and it has failed badly – it seems that you have missed the point entirely	This is a real blow but the situation is certainly easily remedied. Take up the offer of a tutorial as soon as possible. In the meantime make some notes in which you think about exactly what it is that you need help with – is it the question, the writing or the topic itself? Prepare for the tutorial thoroughly and take the assignment along to make notes on as you talk about it.

Your relationship with your tutor breaks down – you can't stand each other

Adopt a polite but a little distant attitude to the tutor – you don't need to go over the top with gushing warmth – and ask for an appointment to see him. In the meeting be as conciliatory as possible and start by admitting that you may have been giving off negative signals and explain what it is that he does that you find difficult to cope with. Remove the blame from either party and talk about 'mixed messages' and the fact that the 'communication has got a bit tricky'. Be specific about what you feel is undermining: 'I find it difficult to work when a tutor doesn't make eye contact – I know it sounds a bit funny' will shame most tutors into making the eye contact without you risking a lowered self-esteem. Use language to diffuse the situation – don't raise the stakes. Don't cry and don't keep bringing the conversation back to what you want – try to see it from the other person's point of view. If all else fails grit your teeth, smile sweetly and make a note to choose an option that he will not be teaching the next time around.

You have a bust up with the group – a class discussion descends into chaos when the whole group tell you that you are in the wrong about something

This is horrible and it takes a lot of courage to recover from. Usually the group will reflect on the fact that things have gone a bit far afterwards. Don't cry or run out of the room, just state your case and, if you are getting nowhere, be quiet. In the next session ask the tutor for some time in which you can explain that you feel a bit hurt and acknowledge that you may have expressed things badly but ask them to respect your opinions even if they don't agree with you.

You have formed a block about a subject – you just don't understand a word about it in the classes and you dread doing the assignment

Other members of the group are your best bet in this situation. Try to get a few people together for a coffee to talk it through. If this doesn't work ask your tutor for a tutorial before things get any worse.

You are so behind with all your work that you can't see any way of catching up

Construct yourself a study plan for the next month or two – using the table earlier in the chapter as a guideline. Write formally to your tutor apologizing for your late submissions, explaining why this has happened and referring her to your plan of remedial action (which you will have attached). Ask for her advice about what to do next.

The decision to withdraw

Sometimes things will get so bad that the decision to suspend or even to terminate your studies needs be taken seriously. A complete break is the only sensible option in certain circumstances. A recent research report (Nutt et al., 2005) has found that dropping out usually happens for more than one reason. Students live complicated and demanding lives and dropping out comes from a combination of accumulated issues, such as lack of funds, feeling isolated, being on the wrong course and lack of support at home as well as the often overwhelming demands of work and family responsibilities. The study found that there are critical pressure points and it is worth bearing these in mind if you are feeling low. These pressure points are arrival at university, the beginning of the second year, key assessment points such as the submission of the first assignment and significant external life events such as a relationship breakdown and the change of work circumstances. It is important that you do not regard the decision to withdraw either temporarily or permanently as a failure on either your part or that of the institution. Many 'drop outs' do eventually return to learning when the time is right and there is no need to write off a rich experience simply because you did not finish within conventional time scales.

Further Reading

- There are plenty of books available that deal explicitly with study skills – with more detailed guidelines about reading and writing at a higher level. Christine Ritchie and Paul Thomas's excellent *Successful Study: Skills for Teaching Assistants* (London: David Fulton, 2004) is aimed directly at adults in the UK working towards teaching assistant qualifications but it has a good deal of information that will be valuable to all adult learners. You might also look at Peter Redman's *Good Essay Writing: A Social Sciences Guide* (London: Sage 2005).

- To read more about patterns of retention of adult learners see Nutt, D. et al., *Retaining Non-Traditional Students in Higher Education*, University of Teesside – Report for the European Social Fund (quoted by Huw Richards in *Guardian*, 7 June 2005).

- Bell, J., *Doing Your Research Project: A Guide for First Time Researchers in Education and Social Science* (Buckingham: Open University Press, 1999) is an accessible, useful book that will help with research projects.

- Alfrey, C., *Understanding Children's Learning* (London: David Fulton, 2003). You may find this book useful because it contains a number of chapters that deal with different aspects of pedagogy. It will be of use to you particularly if you are studying in the field of education or if you are in a more general field but would like to know more about educational theory.

9 Staying the Course: The Resilient Learner in Action

This chapter will:

- Explain the characteristics of reflective and resilient learning and explore the behaviour of the resilient learner
- Give advice for how you can link your reflective approach to learning to your career development
- Explore the ways that you can make the most of your learning when you are applying for jobs and promotions – including how to describe your learning on an application and how to talk about it in an interview situation

Reflective learning

We have talked throughout the book about the necessity of reflecting on work done in an ongoing way. So what does 'reflection' actually mean? Learning can be divided into superficial and profound levels. The surface levels of learning refer to all the things that you learn because you need to know them in the short term but that you forget pretty quickly afterwards. Last-minute cramming for an examination comes into this category of learning. By contrast, more profound learning describes any relatively permanent changes in the way that we perceive ourselves and our environment as a result of some sort of intervention. In other words, this is the sort of learning that happens as a result of a completely new understanding of a subject that you thought you knew, or a complete change in the way that you do something. It could be argued that there is a hierarchy of learning types and that deep learning is always superior. It is worth remembering, though, that what is more important is that you understand the demands of a task and learn it in the most appropriate way. It is not really necessary to have a full understanding of a few lines of a sketch that you and friends are performing for the Christmas party at work – you simply need to know them well enough to be able to walk on and perform. If you were to take a medium-sized part in a production of *The Tempest*, though, for a whole season, of course a much deeper understanding of Shakespeare's lines and theatricality would be appropriate. Deep learning is about transformation; surface learning adds to your repertoire of skills or body of knowledge. Reflective learning happens when the learner recognizes the difference and is able to critically analyze why either state has been achieved. In this way the reflective learner is able to think not just about the content of what has been learned but also about the processes involved in learning about it. The reflective learner thinks explicitly about her own role in the success or failure of the activity and is able to substitute alternative strategies in future situations as a result of this analysis.

The more responsibility that the learner can take for his or her own learning the more effective the learning will be.

Becoming a resilient learner

In order to be a resilient learner you need to understand that learning will always be difficult at times and it is as much about recognizing and celebrating the challenge as it is about enjoying the easier aspects. It is very important to recognize that *learning is supposed to be difficult*. It is not acceptable to expect it to be something you easily slip into. If you do not go up a level, then you are not really doing something that is worthwhile. In my experience of working with successful, resilient adult learners, I have noted that they all share a common approach to learning, even though they may be very different personalities. They see themselves as completers because they hold strongly to the notion that they finish what they begin and this gives them an innate understanding of the progress they are making, even when they go through negative stages. They are often perpetual learners, moving from one activity to the next, through formal and informal phases and as such they see learning something new as being intrinsic to their lives. Common to all these resilient learners is the understanding that anxiety always accompanies the entry to a new field or area of knowledge and moving up a level in the same field. Unlike less resilient learners they are able to withstand this anxiety because they put a good deal of faith in the fact that more secure, comfortable phases will always follow. Finally, they tell me that they have at least one person in their lives who they can trust to absorb their doubts and vulnerabilities and who can support them relentlessly. For some this is a tutor or librarian and for others it is an excellent course administrator. Sometimes that support comes in the form of somebody close who may, or may not be, a learner themselves in a formal sense.

The resilient learner then is one who:

- **Takes criticism seriously but not personally**

- **Sees the learning as life-enhancing rather than a trial**

- **Can see the bigger picture and views the difficult periods as only temporary**

- **Has a deep and genuine belief in the good that can come from learning**

- **Understands that learning needs to be a challenge as well as enjoyable**

- **Enjoys the structure that learning brings to his or her life, rather than just seeing it as an 'add on'**

- **Greets the changes that learning brings with enthusiasm**

- **Understands that learning is about risk-taking and deliberately pursues risk but does so in a supported way by breaking down the risks to achievable components – just signing up for one term rather than a whole year's course in a difficult subject, for example**

- **Accepts that all deep-level learning will involve some degree of anxiety because change is involved but is not put off by that anxiety, rather rides through it using a variety of methods to calm down**

- **Can operate in introvert and extravert ways of working.**

The expected and unexpected outcomes of learning

You will remember that early on in the book we explored the notions of extrinsic and intrinsic motivation. You were encouraged to recognize where your motivation is coming from and to develop to some degree the other type of motivation. So, if your motivation begins as being purely intrinsic you might want to think about what some of the possible material benefits of learning might be, while if you are extrinsically motivated you might try to see the pleasure of learning for its own sake.

A big motivational factor for a lot of people is career advancement. This might be quantified in the form of money or it might simply be about gaining more fulfilment at work. Although a lot of people delight in the fact that the learning provides them with a wonderful escape from the working world (and good for you if this is the case – there is no need to shoehorn in extrinsic motivation if you do not feel it and can do quite well without it), for others the learning provides an extra incentive to keep going when things get difficult as well as a new incentive to progress at work, perhaps after feeling disillusioned for a while.

If you do want to make the connection between learning and work, the following section offers some ideas you might want to put into practice.

Linking professional learning to career development

Some courses clearly have an impact on your working life – a degree in business studies or qualifications directly linked to the work you do are the most obvious examples. It may surprise you, though, that many employers regard any type of learning as an important asset in a work colleague. Companies and organizations are now encouraged to take their arrangements for training and development very seriously. You may even be able to access some funding to help you to continue with your studies. (Useful sources of funding are Learn Direct and the DfES – see the websites given in the further reading section of Chapter 1). A lot depends on how you present your learning interests at work. Think about the transferable skills you have gained from your learning that will be useful in the work environment. These include:

- **The ability to take on new information rapidly**

- **Writing and presentation skills**

- **The ability to apply new understanding to familiar situations.**

Promoting your present and current achievements on an application form

Whether you have chosen to follow a vocational course or not, it is always a good idea to emphasize what you have learned on application forms and letters of application.

The main point of the letter that accompanies your application form is to get you noticed, so use your experience of learning to help your application to stand out.

Try to point out the barriers you have overcome in order to learn effectively and the skills that you have developed in order to complete your course. It is worth stressing how you have juggled your priorities and the way that your concentration skills have developed. Explain how you have been able to keep up with work commitments, or, if you have not been working, explain how the experience of studying has led you to think that you would like to get back into the work market.

It helps to express what you have learned in wide terms that make sense to people not 'inside' the discipline in the same way that you are. So, instead of saying 'I did a course about *Wuthering Heights* and *Jane Eyre*' you might write something like 'I have enjoyed learning about nineteenth-century literature and I find the work of the Brontes particularly interesting'. It is a case of giving your reader enough information to make them interested in what you are saying but keeping it wide enough so that they understand the depth and breadth of your knowledge. In the same way, when explaining about your Introduction to the History of Art course, in which you have done your specialist essay on the art of Andy Warhol, you could say 'I am studying the History of Art and I have made a particular study of twentieth-century North American art'. Employers get so many bland and boring application forms that you will be surprised by how much interest they show in this sort of thing. The whole point of the application form is that it is a device to get you an interview. You do not need to go overboard with information at this stage – just give them enough to whet their appetites!

Talking about your learning in an interview situation

Assuming that your pithy but interesting application form has worked, the next step is to think about how you will present yourself as a learner in the interview situation. The trick here is to draw from your learning experiences enough to show your prospective employers that you are an intelligent, lively and interesting person but at the same time to convince them that you are not so enthralled with your studies that you are likely to be drawn away from the job that they are (hopefully) about to offer you.

Be enthusiastic about your subject – even if it is not directly linked to the job or position for which you are applying. When asked directly about your learning (these will often be the 'warm up' questions when the interviewers are trying to get a handle on what sort of person you are) feel free to speak with liveliness and enthusiasm. In other questions – when the interviewers ask you about the qualities that you will bring to the job, for example – try to draw on the experience of the learning to give examples of your assets as a worker. So, you might say that you are able to think deeply and to view all aspects of the situation before you commit yourself to an action and that this has been born out of your experience of looking at topics that you have written and read about.

If your course is directly linked to the job that you are applying for then try to show with your answers that you have internalized the knowledge – almost that you would have known it anyway. So instead of saying 'We have done stuff on special needs education on the course …' try saying 'There are competing views about inclusion and special needs in education and the most recent work suggests that …'. In other words, you want to make it clear that you have a deep understanding of the issues and that you will bring this level of knowledge to your new post.

Finally, if you know that your prospective employer has recently gained an Investor in People award (which recognizes its commitment to the ongoing learning of its workforce) then you might make a point that this is what has attracted you to the employer because it links to your own personal commitment to lifelong learning.

Using learning to plan career advancement or career change

In the first chapter we looked at the evidence that suggests that people who engage in learning in their adult years are more likely than their economic and social equivalents to earn higher salaries. One of the common responses for embarking on learning in adult life is that it makes us reappraise what it is that we want from life and helps us to gain a new understanding of where our strengths lie. Think about the way that the learning has transformed you as a person and allow it to lead you in the directions that you will enjoy and benefit from. You might find, for example, that working on your own writing projects and assignments has convinced you that the highly sociable career you had previously is less appealing.

Try to think strategically before you make a move. Think about your current occupation and lifestyle. Make a list of all the things that are in it already that you value and the ones that you like the least. Try not to make the mistake of thinking that in the new career everything will be completely different – elements may well cross over and re-emerge in a different form. If you currently work in retail, for example, and you love meeting and helping people but hate the financial spreadsheets that you have to deal with, then you can bet quite safely that your imagined career in teaching will have a good deal of the former but hardly any of the latter (unless you want to move into management). If it is the rigid way that your time at work is managed in the shop – so that you can only take coffee breaks at pre-ordained times – that bothers, you then think carefully before you make a move to teaching. Time in a school is also highly regulated and you may find that after a while the things that bother you in your new career are the same as those that bothered you in your old one. If this is the case then you might want to think more laterally about your planned move. Perhaps working in further or adult education might suit you better. A staged move that capitalizes on your existing skills will always be less threatening than a dramatic move to a completely new arena.

Taking responsibility for your own independent learning

We have spent much of this book examining the ways in which you will work with tutors and other students, but actually by far the majority of the work that you will do in the pursuit of your studies will be done by yourself. Try to see yourself as the main agent for your learning – the tutors are there to help but you have ultimate responsibility for your progress. Use the following motivational tricks to stay on course when you find keeping yourself going rather challenging.

- **We tend to stick at things more readily when there is an emotional payback for us. It goes without saying that the parts of your study programme that you enjoy** the most are the ones that you are most likely to work hardest at (and this will link to your strongest learning style preference), while those things that you find most difficult will be the ones that you spend the least time on. So try to attach a reward to those things that you might find the most difficult – a walk in the sunshine as a payback for 40 minutes' concentrated work on an assignment, say, or a glass of wine as a reward for an evening spent reading about a topic that does not interest you much.

- **Fool your mind with language.** We used to think that language merely reflected meaning that is already there – so we say 'I feel anxious' when we feel the butterflies in our tummies and the racing heart. But it is also true that language can create meaning. So, you might say 'I feel nervous' when you feel very calm but to all intents and purposes, as far as all the people listening to you are concerned, you are nervous – because you have said so (this is a traditional way of getting your audience to sympathize with you, by the way). So you could try the reverse psychology trick of using positive words to describe an activity that you might otherwise dread. It will feel ridiculous at first, but by saying out loud (to yourself or to your friends or family) 'I'm really looking forward to doing this section of the assignment today' or 'It will be nice to get into college and meet everyone else again' when all you really want to do is lie in bed for the rest of the day, can work a treat!

- **Anticipate setbacks because they will happen.** Some people are hopelessly thrown off course by events that others would only regard as an unavoidable nuisance. Illnesses, problems with the car, computer problems and so on are all part of life and you can pretty much predict that they will always hit at the time when they are most disruptive. So take account of this when you are planning your study schedules and make time for things that may go wrong. If and when they do, try not to let them derail your whole programme by putting them in the wider perspective.

- **Making a work schedule that is written down can help enormously.** You could do this electronically by making a calendar with all the important deadlines entered, or you could do it by creating a timetable for yourself – cheap diaries bought in the January sales are great for this. By physically making a note of your expectations you will imprint these ideas on your brain as well as having something to refer to as a way of keeping you on track.

- **Avoid procrastination.** Always try to do the thing that you are least happy about as early on in the day as your body clock will allow you to in order to do it well. This has the double bonus of getting the job done and at the same time you can incorporate the motivational benefits of the reward by promising yourself something that you want to do (going swimming/shopping) as a reward once it is done.

- Accept that we all have bad days. It is inexplicable why on some days we are able to work away at a cracking pace, writing huge numbers of words of good quality or reading through an enormous amount of text, while on others even just writing a sentence can seem like getting blood from the proverbial stone. There are countless reasons for this – the weather, tiredness, your hormones, disturbances, whatever. The main thing to do is to see these 'off' days from the long view. When it is really not working, then give up and take a break. Use the time to do something you would have to do anyway – go to the supermarket or take the dog for a walk or do some laundry. You will nearly always find that you work better the next day and that the break has refreshed you.

- Rewards and praise work well to keep you motivated but just the right amount of negative emotion can also be a motivator. The looming deadline can work wonders to get a project finished and many people swear that they can only really work well when they are up against a series of externally imposed deadlines. Too much negative emotion can have the opposite effect though and we can literally become paralysed with fear or feelings of desolation because the task in hand is simply too enormous. Work out how much positive and negative emotion you need to spur you on and use it to your own advantage.

So there you have it. These ideas should help you to maintain your motivation for study and help you to work to your best capacity. You have spent most of your life gaining the confidence to do this, so now go ahead and enjoy it.

Further Reading

- Dr Raj Persaud writes in depth about the idea of resilience and the concept that is often linked to resilience – hardiness – in relation to mental health in his 1997 book *Staying Sane: How to Make Your Mind Work for You* (London: Metro Books). He says (p. 13), 'The mentally healthy person doesn't necessarily sail through their divorce, sacking or bereavement, but is less prone to a nervous breakdown on such occasions … In other words, mentally healthy people are able to learn emotionally from whatever life throws at them.'

- Guy Claxton's excellent book *Wise Up: Learning to Love the Learning Life* (Stafford: Network Educational Press, 1999) will help you to develop your understanding of the links between your self, your learning and your life in a more theoretical context.

Bibliography

Alfrey, C. (2003) *Understanding Children's Learning*. London: David Fulton.

Bell, J. (1999) *Doing Your Research Project: A Guide for First Time Researchers in Education and Social Science*. Buckingham: Open University Press.

Benton, D. (1996) *Food for Thought: How What You Eat Affects Your Mood, Memory and Thinking*. Harmondsworth: Penguin.

Brealey, E. (2004) *The Spirit of Meditation*. London: Cassell Illustrated.

Butt, T. and Burr, V. (2004) *Invitation to Personal Construct Psychology*, 2nd ed. London and Philadelphia: Whurr.

Buzan, Tony (1974) *Use your Head*. London: BBC Books.

Claxten, G. (1999) *Wise Up: Learning to Live the Learning, Life*. Stafford, UK: Network Educational Press.

HH the Dalai Lama (Bstan-'Dzin-Rgya-Mtsho) (2000) *Transforming the Mind: Teachings on Generating Compassions*. London: Thorsons.

Day, M. (2000) in Wangberg, J.K. and Nelson, J.V., *The Ellbogen Experience: Essays on Teaching by Award-Winning University of Wyoming Faculty – Laranne*. Wyoming, University of Wyoming. pp. 67–82.

Dewey, J. (1963) *Experience and Education*. New York: Collier Books (first published in 1938).

Domar, Alice D. and Dreher, Henry (1996) *Healthy Mind, Healthy Woman*. New York: Henry Holt.

Dubin, P. (1962) *Human Relations in Administration*. Englewood Cliffs, NJ: Prentice Hall.

Dunn, K. and Dunn, R. (1978) *Teaching Students through Their Individual Learning Styles*. Englewood Cliff, NJ: Prentice Hall.

Entwistle, N.J. (1988) *Styles of Learning and Teaching*. London: David Fulton.

Feinstein, L. and Hammond, C. (2004) 'The Contribution of Adult Learning to Health and Social Capital', *The Oxford Review of Education*, 30(2): 199–221.

Ford, G. (2005) *Am I Still Needed? Guidance and Learning for Older Adults*. Derby: Centre for Guidance Studies (CEGS).

Gale, C. and Martyn, C. (1998) 'Larks and Owls and Health, Wealth and Wisdom', *British Medical Journal*, 317: 1675–1677.

Gardner, H. (1993) *Frames of Mind: The Theory of Multiple Intelligences*. London: Fontana Press.

Gardner, H. (1999) *Intelligence Reframed: Multiple Intelligences for the 21st Century*. New York: Basic Books.

Goleman, D. (1998) *Working with Emotional Intelligence*. London: Bloomsbury.

Greenberger, D. and Padesky, C. (1995) *Mind Over Mood: Change How You Feel by Changing the Way that You Think*. New York: Guilford Press.

Hammond, C. (2002) *Learning to be Healthy*. London: Centre for Research on the Wider Benefits of Learning, Birkbeck College.

Honey, P. and Mumford, A. (1986) *The Manual of Learning Styles*. Maidenhead: Peter Honey Publications.

Honey, P. and Mumford, A. (2000) *The Learning Styles Helper's Guide*. Maidenhead: Peter Honey Publications.

Hughes, D., Bosley, S., Bowes, L. and Bysshe, S. (2002) *The Economic Benefits of Guidance*. Derby: Centre for Guidance Studies (CEGS).

James, K. (2001) *Prescriptions for Learning: Evaluation Report*. Leicester: National Institute for Adult Continuing Education.

James, Oliver (2002) *They F*** You Up: How to Survive Family Life*. London: Bloomsbury.

Jung, C. (1977) *Psychological Types,* trans. R.F.C. Hull. *Collected Works of Carl Jung*, vol. 6, Bollingen Series XX. Princeton, NJ: Princeton University Press.

Kelly, G. (1955) *The Psychology of Personal Constructs*, vols 1 and 2. New York: W.W. Norton.

Knowles, M.S. (1980) *The Modern Practice of Adult Education: From Andragogy to Pedagogy*. Chicago: Follett Publishing.

Kolb, David A. (1978/1983) *Learning Style Inventory*. Boston, MA: McBer.

Kolb, David A. (1984) *Experiential Learning: Experience as the Source of Learning and Development*. Upper Saddle River, NJ: Prentice Hall.

Lewis, Ivan (2005) Interview with Ellie Levenson. *New Statesman*, 25 March, p. xii.

Lindeman, E. (1989) *The Meaning of Adult Education*. Oklahoma: Oklahoma Research Centre (first published in 1926).

Maslow, A. (1954) *Motivation and Personality*. New York: Harper and Row.

McCarthy, B. (1981) *The 4Mat System: Teaching and Learning Styles with Right/Left Mode Techniques*. Oak Brook ITL: Excel Inc.

Myers Briggs, I. (1962) *The Myers Briggs Type Indicator Manual*. Princeton, NJ: Educational Testing Services.

Nutt, D. et al. (2005) 'Retaining Non-Traditional Students in Higher Education', University of Teesside – report for the European Social Fund. (Quoted by Huw Richards, *Guardian*, 7 June.)

Persaud, Raj (1997) *Staying Sane: How to Make Your Mind Work for You*. London: Metro Books.

Reay, D., Ball, S. and David, M. (2002) 'It's taking me a long time but I'll get there in the end: mature students on access courses and higher education choice', *British Education Research Journal*, 28 (1), pp. 5–21.

Redman, P. (2005) *Good Essay Writing: A Social Sciences Guide*, 3rd edn. London: Sage.

Riding, R.J. (1994) *Cognitive Styles Analysis*. Birmingham: Learning and Training Technology.

Riding, R. and Rayner, S. (1998) *Cognitive Styles and Learning Strategies: Understanding Style Differences in Learning and Behaviour*. London: David Fulton.

Ritchie, C. and Thomas, P. (2004) *Successful Study: Skills for Teaching Assistants*. London: David Fulton.

Rose, C. (1985) *Accelerated Learning*. New York: Dell.

Rowe, D. (1993) *The Successful Self*. New York: HarperCollins.

Rowe, D. (2002) *Beyond Fear*. New York: HarperCollins.

Sansone, Carole and Harackiewicz, J.M. (eds) (2000) *Intrinsic and Extrinsic Motivation: The Search for Optimal Motivation and Performance*. San Diego, CA: Academic Press, esp. chapter by R.M. Ryan and E.L. Deci, 'When rewards compete with nature: the undermining of intrinsic motivation and self-regulation'.

Schon, D. (1983) *The Reflective Practitioner: How Professionals Think in Action*. San Fransisco: Jossey-Bass.

Watkins, C., Carnell, E., Lodge, C. (1996) *Effective Learning*, National School Improvement Network's 'Research Matters' series. London: Institute of Education.

West, L. (1996) *Beyond Fragments: Adults, Motivation and Higher Education*. London: Taylor and Francis.

Zohar, D. and Marshall, I. (2000) *Spiritual Intelligence: The Ultimate Intelligence*. London: Bloomsbury.

Index

Indexed by Caroline Eley